MW00365704

SHOCK THE TOPLINE

Robby,

Above all esle, you are Chief Growth Officer. This is a book that covers a lot of ground. It cover topics that are essential to you and your agency's growth.

You've made great strides in the short time I've known you. Now onto growth!

Dan

SHOCK THE TOPLINE

A PRACTICAL GUIDE FOR GROWING YOUR INSURANCE PRACTICE

David E Estrada

Copyright © 2016 David E Estrada
All rights reserved.

ISBN: 0692664327
ISBN 13: 9780692664322
Library of Congress Control Number: 2016935709
Rainmaker Advisory LLC, Portland, OR

For My Father, Robert Emmet Estrada

TABLE OF CONTENTS

PREFACE

This book is intended for insurance professionals who wish to achieve more success and advance their careers. A career in the insurance profession is both extremely rewarding and fulfilling as its overall mission is to serve others and protect the social fabric. From my experience, it is a truly worthwhile pursuit and one of the noble professions. Yet this career comes with great demands; many challenges must be endured and steep obstacles overcome in order to achieve the desired outcomes for your practice and career overall.

Unfortunately, a great deal of the content and training programs offered to insurance professionals focuses on what to do and seldom includes how to actually do it. Why? Because those offering this content and providing these programs have no actual experience, much less accomplishments in, the subject matter. Furthermore, many of these programs focus on learning pop psychology or linguistic trickery, and often you'll find that authors, trainers, and self-described experts are providing nothing more than general sales theory offered up in the newest shiny box.

I have written this book because I love the profession, I believe it is important and significant to society, and there are great people out there who care about it and are struggling to succeed. I am disturbed that the content and training programs available for professional development fall short and lead producers astray in so many respects. And, tragically, this "training" is costing great people their careers.

This book will highlight what to do to grow your insurance practice as well as recommendations and options for how to do it with methods that have actually been proven as valid and effective in the field. You will see content that is from my own experience, the experience of others in this field who have been successful, and even experiences of the clients we work with in real time here at Rainmaker—which means this is fresh content and applicable to your practice today!

You'll find three sections in this book: the first providing an overall perspective of the industry and considerations that will help you navigate your career; the second focusing on topline growth; and the third for existing sales leaders to provide more value to producers as well as for producers who want to migrate into leadership. At the end of each chapter you'll find questions to ask yourself. I am hoping that these questions will become part of your calendars to remind you of important items to focus your efforts upon throughout your year, as well as fodder for roundtable discussions among producer peer groups or even for discussions moderated by leadership in sales meetings.

I focus the second section on topline growth. Why? Because it's been my experience that advancing an insurance practice should start there, and it allows some breathing room to circle back on operational and other "back-end" issues that are also tied to growth. Addressing back-end issues can make a dramatic impact on the growth of an insurance practice—yet given most circumstances, it's challenging to focus on those key drivers when there simply isn't enough money coming in the door and you're stressed out because you're hanging on by your fingernails trying to survive! So this book will help you "shock the topline" and generate more revenue—after which you can circle back to operational, process, workflow, and other skills as you deem appropriate to continue the growth of your practice. Let's get started!

SECTION 1: PERSPECTIVE

CHAPTER 1

GOVERNING PRINCIPLES AND KEY STRATEGIES FOR BOOK GROWTH

G rowth is a career-long pursuit, and growing your book is critical for any producer of any tenure classification. This chapter will examine the five governing principles of book growth: client retention, account rounding and cross-selling, new account acquisition, center-of-influence and strategic-alliance-partner development, and the development of sales initiatives. We'll also examine strategies behind growth, defining the ideal prospect, the value of research, and whether or not you should write larger cases progressively throughout your career or simply more of the same.

The Five Governing Principles

Principle #1: Client Retention
Client retention is paramount. You can't grow your book of business if you're losing clients. Consistency and continuity are critical for higher retention. One of the critical components of increasing client retention is developing a twelve-month service calendar or game plan. These identify what you will do, when it will be done, and who will do it. I recommend doing this for any client, but especially for your top ten clients, as they are often being courted by other brokers and being asked what their broker is doing about X, Y, and Z. For this reason providing an

annual service calendar goes a long way to preventing competitors from exploiting missing elements of what you are providing in terms of an annual service plan, or even the absence of a plan being deployed, to acquire your client!

Social interaction is a key element that contributes to client retention and should not be underestimated. One of the benefits of social interaction is that is allows you to capture important nuances of information that don't necessarily lend themselves to formal business discussions and common business etiquette protocols. For example, in a formal business setting when your primary buyer is with their work peers at the table, they may feel uncomfortable in revealing certain aspects of the firm's culture or issues that are material for you to know in helping you generate a happy client over the long term. A lunch, a dinner, or even just a morning coffee creates the opportunity for an informal exchange. Such discussions can help you understand some of the entity's political nuances that will help you both serve and preserve the client over the long term.

Finally, take time to understand those individuals with a stake in your services 360 degrees around your primary buyer. So in addition to your primary buyer, who are the stakeholders around them that can weigh in on a given decision? What is their agenda? What's important to them? How can you help your primary buyer successfully address the questions those stakeholders may have? Your buyer has people to please within their organization, so helping them deal with stakeholder concerns and preparing them for those discussions is not only key to client retention over time but also contributes to the process of new client acquisition.

Principle #2: Account Rounding and Cross-Selling

Keep in mind that many relationships are substantively formed during the immediacy of a sales transaction, which can leave many boxes unchecked. Frequently what happens is that there is a long courtship period—a year, or even two or three—but when they are ready to make a move, they require that your work be done very quickly in order to secure their business. When that happens, many boxes can be left unchecked. Doing a quarterly sweep of your accounts can address this issue. Have you written all the lines of coverage? Have they been introduced to the other side of the house? What is missing that needs to be fulfilled during the course of a sustainable relationship?

Many buyers don't "give you the baby" right away; they intentionally start small and see how you perform before trusting you with greater opportunities for engagement with other lines of coverage. These quarterly sweeps, looking for gaps and new opportunities, can be a significant contributor to higher retention because the more lines of coverage that you write for a given client, the higher the retention rate.

I have heard many brokers say that they want the whole thing or not at all, but I believe that's foolish. I believe that it's important to be patient and not draw any lines in the sand in terms of writing their business. It's okay to establish yourself in terms of one or two lines of coverage, and then based on your performance throughout the year, you can vie for the other pieces of business as the relationship develops. This is especially important in cross-sell business because of the very nature of the introduction from someone that already holds business with that client—essentially, you don't want to embarrass the person referring their client to you by taking an extreme position in terms of wanting all their coverages or none at all!

Principle # 3: Converting "non-Clients" into Clients

This is the most critical principle of book growth that defines a successful broker. At the end of the day, the ability to convert non-clients into clients is the key to being a successful producer over the course of your career. If you can do this, everything else will tend to fall into place, so this is a key area to focus your skills. A significant yet often dismissed contributor to new client generation is the sheer act of research. Researching a prospect takes minutes and will allow you to see things that can help you make a more impactful approach. Specifics are everything here. You want them to feel like your approach was specific to them and their circumstances. That's what will differentiate you and help you gain greater access to potential clients versus those using a canned, one-size-fits-all approach or using some sort of linguistic formula, pop psychology, or other trickery intended to manipulate someone into a conversation.

Focusing on niche situations or buyer properties is a hallmark of top-performing producers. Generalists tend to stall out over time, ultimately achieving a book of about $300,000 to $400,000 in annual revenue. We know as a fact that most producers with million-dollar books and above tend to focus on niches, specific situations, or buyer properties. Of course most of us start our careers with an anything-and-everything prospecting methodology. Most of us will write business with people who we know and have known for a while, regardless of whether they own a plumbing store, a bakery, or a machine shop. But we know that books like that ultimately flatten out at about $300,000 to $400,000 of annualized revenue; to go beyond that, it's important to focus on some specific niches in order to sustain the growth of your practice over time.

As you move upmarket, understanding the roles and concerns of different stakeholders becomes more important for success. Main Street businesses are typically characterized by one highly empowered buyer, whether it's the business owner or the office manager. But, when we move upmarket, transactions are often defined by the fact that there is more than one stakeholder in the buying process. Therefore, understanding the roles and concerns of the different stakeholders involved in the buying process is more important for success with mid-market businesses than it is with Main Street businesses.

When you're competing for Main Street business, it can feel like everyone and their brother owns an insurance agency or knows an insurance agent, so the competition is broad. In mid-market, you will probably only see five to ten prevailing brokers competing with you for that business. Tracking them, whether it's via auto-notification from a search engine or by following their company pages on LinkedIn® professional networking services, will help you keep abreast of what those competitors are doing and help you maintain a competitive stance within your market.

I encourage targeting large accounts by how long it will take you to make up for it if you lose them. I know this is a somewhat unorthodox concept and position to raise for most readers—however, doing so is prudent in the long term. Would it be six to twelve months or longer of your typical annual new business production to make up for losing one of your largest accounts? Some producers evaluate this issue by examining it in terms of a factor of their largest current account, whether it's a multiple of 1.5 or 2.0 or 3.0. For example, imagine your new business run rate is $100,000 of new business per year, and by happenstance, you write a $200,000 commission case. It's important to understand that if you lose that case, it will take you roughly two years to make up for it. Many producers like to chase progressively larger pieces of business, and of course writing progressively larger pieces of business is the key to sustainable organic growth over time, but just be sure to keep your eyes open and understand the time it will take you to make up the business if you lose it. Use caution. Don't forget that your client management team, who may be more familiar with managing smaller accounts, may find it difficult or a stretch to manage something much larger and may need development to preserve that business over time. As we all know, it's one thing to write a piece of business, and another thing to keep it!

Principle #4: Strategic-Alliance Partners and Center-of-Influence Development

This type of initiative increases deal flow over time. It compresses the courtship cycle of each specific new client referred because you're leveraging the credibility of the person who is referring you, who has worked with them and established a relationship with them over time. This allows you to duplicate yourself in terms of prospecting activity by orders of magnitude. However, this type of business should be pursued in concert with your active new client development strategy, not in lieu of it.

Over time, the clients you develop from center-of-influence relationships will be quite lucrative, and retention will be high. Center-of-influence and strategic-alliance partners are great in that channel of business for advocacy if relationship friction occurs with a client you hold that they referred to you. For example, if you're delivering a renewal that is significantly larger than last year's premium and you've done the best that you can to work it down, it's great to work that business through the center of influence after you deliver their renewal. As an illustration, you might ask the center of influence, "Did they say anything to you? How upset are they? Are there any flames that I could squelch? Any additional work to keep them happy that's required from your perspective?"

Remember that center-of-influence and strategic-alliance partners contribute to our competitive intelligence—networking opportunities, professional branding, and prestige. In working with them, you may have access to events where your buyers congregate that would not be possible to attend on your own. Attending those events with strategic-alliance partners can help with branding and visibility within the local business community, and of course it can provide access to viable prospects. It's that significant.

Principle #5: Sales Initiatives

These are coordinated outbound marketing efforts designed to acquire specific types of businesses by niche, situation, or buyer characteristics. A sales initiative allows for efficient marshalling of both internal support and enterprise-level support. When I was producing business, the more I defined what I was doing with leadership, the more support I was able to obtain from them for those given initiatives.

For example, if leadership asks about what you want to accomplish and you reply that you simply want to write more business, you will get less support than if you reply with specifics like these: "I want to launch a biotech initiative," or "I want to develop a brown bag lunch initiative where we invite clients and prospects to learn about new elements of legislation," or "I want to work on taking one of the ten largest accounts away from our biggest competitor." The specificity of these initiatives will enable leadership to get their arms around what you're doing and support it much more effectively than a general objective, thereby helping you achieve the results you are seeking.

Growth Strategies

Defining the Ideal Prospect

I have always loved the saying, "An arrow without a target will never hit its mark." A clear definition of your ideal client is key. When we work with an agency's production team, we always start with a diagnostic probing many aspects of how they manage and grow their book of business. A typical shortcoming that is revealed is a fuzzy definition of what they view as an ideal client. Below are typical responses to the question, "How do you define your ideal client?":

- "100 to 500 employees, fully insured."
- "Family owned and humble, looking for a professional."
- "Someone I enjoy working with, loyal, and cares about their employees."
- "Someone who has an issue that we can clean up for them, bring value to."
- "100+ any industry."

We recommend to our clients that they test their ideal client definition along four categories as a best practice. The first is that the definition must be clear. Second, it must be in line with your firm's desired business. Third, it should be in line with your own ability to successfully transact. Fourth, does it enable ease of introductions and referrals because it's easy to remember? For example, suppose you meet an attorney from a large law firm at a social or networking event and they express interest in sending some business your way. You couldn't possibly say, "Here's what we're looking for: a family-owned and humble business, looking for a professional." But if you said, "I'm looking for a high-tech firm, with over fifty employees and growing quickly," that would be a much easier characteristic for the attorney to identify within their own portfolio of clients or known relationships to refer to you. That's what you want to look for in terms of being specific. That degree of specificity helps your contacts assign resources appropriately, more easily garnishes effective support, and enables you to obtain introductions and referrals to people that fit within a specific ideal client definition you desire.

Make Research Work for You

The running start that research provides is everything. It clearly demonstrates that you're a professional, because professionals do research. It differentiates you from the competition during the approach and will increase your chances of securing a first meeting. It will also help you shape your discovery questions, allowing you to not only obtain better information but increasing your viability as an alternative to the incumbent broker. Research will apprise you of material events during the courtship process that may contribute to adjustments or to emphasizing different aspects of your value proposition to increase your chances of securing the business. And remember, research is fast becoming the price of admission for mid-market and large market business.

Before the Internet, you could show up to a meeting and ask somebody, "What do you do for a living?" But now it just takes minutes online to get a sense of the career history of the person that you're talking to which can provide clues to how they buy from vendors and what their preferences might be in doing so. Have they been with large firms and therefore tend to purchase from larger firms? Have they been with smaller firms and tend to purchase from smaller firms? Research enables you to reinforce your approach and make it more impactful and, therefore, more effective.

The Economics of Book Building

Let's talk a little bit about the economics of building out a book out of business. Is it better to write 20 percent more clients each year or to write clients that are 20 percent larger each year? Fundamentally, this is an issue of working smarter versus work harder. In a lot of sales environments the leadership says, "Just write more accounts! If you want to write twice as much business, make twice the calls and book twice the appointments." But this can only get you so far. Inevitably you will hit a peak because there are only so many hours in the day.

When you look at successful producers over time, the reason they've been able to develop a multimillion-dollar book is because they have written progressively larger accounts over time—not more of them! In fact, most multimillion-dollar book producers write significantly fewer accounts per year than they did in the beginning of their career, not more! It comes down to the fact that there are only so many hours in the day. If you're pursuing the course of action of increasing the number of accounts you write by 20 percent year over year, then you're really just making the hamster run faster and faster in his little cage. Eventually he's going to get tuckered out. What you want is to develop techniques, resources, and capabilities to write progressively larger pieces of business that are more complex and, obviously, more lucrative. That's where it's at, because at the end of the day, there is only so much time available.

Pay attention to your new business pipeline's average case. If you are pursuing business that on average is lower than the average size case in your existing book of business, you are actually shrinking your book. If it is larger than the average size case, you are growing your book of business sustainably over time. As you navigate your career over time, always track and compare the average size case in both your existing book of business and your new business pipeline.

Pursuing this course of action—writing progressively larger pieces of business—will require you to work with your team differently and develop leadership and project management skills. You will also need to increase your technical expertise and networking as well as maintain healthy center-of-influence development in addition to many other skills (many of which are highlighted in this book for the reader).

Growth should never stop. If you think you will ever find a spot to rest and coast your way through, I am sorry to have to tell you this, but you've chosen the wrong occupation! If you are resting or just sitting on your book, renewing your clients and not actively pursuing progressively larger accounts, then chances are your book is shrinking and you are essentially putting into play the long-term liquidation of your book.

What can you do? Consider turning your attention to one of the principles of growth described in this chapter that especially resonates with you, and pursue that one first. Then try another and another. Ask yourself the questions that follow to help you identify areas for growth and change.

Questions to Assess Growing Your Book

- Have I asked my account management team to inform me of service successes in real time so I can promote them and leverage for introductions?
- Do I know personal information about the buyers within my top ten clients? Do I know if they like to play golf? Do I know their kids' names? Do I know their pet's name? Do I know what hobbies they like or which sports teams they root for?
- Do I perform a quarterly sweep of my accounts with my team specific to what we've sold to a client and what we have yet to sell to them?
- What vendors are attached to my top ten clients? Who are their CPAs, bankers, and lawyers?
- What is my definition of an ideal client?
- What research do I perform prior to approaching an ideal client?
- Is the average size case in my book of business increasing year over year?
- Is the average size case in my new business pipeline below or above the average size case I have in my book of business?

CHAPTER 2

NAVIGATING YOUR CAREER

I n this chapter, we'll be discussing how to navigate your career within the insurance profession. We'll look at common experiences along a prototypical career path, how priorities change across a career path, and questions to ask yourself along the way based upon where you are within your career. Questions at the end of the chapter will provide a valuable self-assessment tool for you to use. I encourage the reader, regardless of what tenure class in which you currently reside, to read through all of the tenure class traits. Why? Because you may see some things you missed early in your career in terms of skills or milestones that might be holding you back and that you can address in order to move forward.

The First Three Years

The first three years are a trying period of time. The running joke is that when you start in the insurance industry, you take the two-year vow of poverty. I wish that was not true, but evidence, as well as my own personal experience, suggests otherwise. However, there's a compelling case to make that this sacrifice works out in the long run, not only within the insurance profession but in virtually any pursuit for that matter.

Priorities
One of the most critical priorities at this time is to increase the number of people who know who you are and know what you do. Record keeping

is vital. Track who you've spoken with, what the discussion was about, what their expiration date is, who their carrier is, who their broker is, and any gripes they may have.

I also encourage, in this phase of your career, to write virtually any size and type of business you can; use the anything-and-everything marketing strategy early in your career. Doing so will allow you to expand your base broadly across all industries and circumstances. It doesn't matter whether it's a plumbing repair shop, a car dealership, a contractor, an electronic manufacturer, a biotech firm, a high-tech business, or a trucking company. Write as much as you can and experience as much as you can in this phase of your development. This will compress your learning curve and accelerate your ability to gain more experience, which will lead to writing a large book sooner than someone starting in a specific niche or industry and having a narrower experience early on in their career.

Attend every live event you can and rub elbows with everyone, whether it's a chamber of commerce mixer, a specific industry mixer, a nonprofit fundraising event, or an association that governs or caters to specific industry classifications. Go! Show up! Shake hands! Increase the number of people who know who you are and know what you do.

Another way to help yourself accomplish a successful transition through this phase of your career is to construct some games you can play. One of my earliest coaches said that if you can reach twelve people a day, you'll have a good career. He encouraged me to keep twelve pennies on my desk; he said every time I reached a potential buyer of insurance, introduced myself, and asked them if I could have a meeting, I could take a penny off my desk. The point was to get all the pennies off my desk by the end of the day.

I had another coach who encouraged me to pursue leads by starting each week with twenty-five rubber bands on the visor of my car. The idea was to keep my eyes open for leads while I was in my car—whether I was driving and noticed a business name on a truck, or a billboard, or the logo of a firm on a building. Basically I was looking for anything that I could pursue. I would go back to my office, perform research, and then reach out to them for an appointment. For each "lead" I discovered while in my car, I'd snap a rubber band off the visor. My job was to get twenty-five of those rubber bands off of my visor by the end of the week. Every Monday morning before I drove to work, I'd put the twenty-five rubber bands back on the visor for the upcoming week. It actually worked very well for me and generated a lot of activity and some good new business.

Constructing activity games helped me build my business early on, and they can for you too if you use them faithfully. But another benefit is that they can help carry you through those times when everything feels dark and depressing. Games allow you to see that you are working and moving forward and doing what you can to make real progress during those dark and gloomy periods that exist in between securing new clients.

Another critical aspect of this time in your career is feeding your brain. Subscribe to everything: blogs, podcasts, and online networking groups. You can also pursue a professional designation during this time. The "benefit" of not yet having a significant book that requires your attendance and time in servicing a lot of clients is the time available for forward-oriented activity, including education and pursuing professional designations. Use that time wisely.

Most of your business in this phase will come from relationships, observation, cold canvassing, and cold calling. Through it all, I encourage you to keep the faith, work hard, and mind your expenses, which often involves things like learning different ways to cook noodles for dinner when you get home!

Here are some questions to ask yourself in this phase:

- *What am I doing to increase the number of people who know who I am and know what I do?* That is the foundation of this career phase, so attending to that is important.
- *What am I doing to record my discussions and collect expiration dates and renewal information so I can follow up in the future on a timely basis?*
- *What events do I attend where my buyers congregate?*
- *What are my buyers reading that I'm reading as well?* It's important to learn about your buyers' minds, and an easy way to do so is simply ask, "What do you read? What blogs do you read? What white papers do you read? What magazines do you subscribe to?" Read those, because that gives you a sense of your buyers' preferences

and concerns so that you can match that and serve those prefer- ences and concerns in your discussions with them.

- *What industry designations am I pursuing?* This is an ideal time to pursue a GBA, a CEBS, a CIC, a CPCU, or an ARM, just to name a few. If you're able to secure at least one designation during this period of time, that's considered a success. This also helps take away the objection, "This person is new, so do they know what they're doing?" Having a designation while competing with a veteran who does not have one can help tip the odds in your favor in many cases.

Three to Five Years

During the three-to-five-year mark, you start to get the feeling of be- ing in a rhythm. There is also the formation of a sales process, and the fact that others can see that you've survived those initial years and now they're beginning to take a more earnest look at you to do business with than before.

Priorities

An important priority now is to master the pipeline. This will be a lifeline for your practice throughout your career. Best practice is to update it at least once a week.

I have to confess that during this point in my career I really defied the idea of doing a pipeline. I didn't want to do it or think about it or update it. I felt sales was intuitive and difficult to quantify. An early men- tor of mine helped me turn a corner in my career by saying, "David, you're right. Sales is intuitive, but the business of sales is not." That's what clicked for me as an insurance professional, and that's the point in time when I began diligently completing a pipeline and doing other ac- tivities that served the business side of growing a book of business. Doing so helped catapult my career forward by orders of magnitude.

Intuition will certainly serve you well, but it is not enough. Leadership needs empirical data, a plan, a structure, and a template.

Every producer should be able to run a projection on their book of business. Based on how much you're writing today (if your new business run rate is, for example, $180,000, and your book is at half a million), where will you be three years from now? Four years from now? Five years from now? How much new business are you adding each year? How much are you losing through normal retention or attrition? How much staff allocation do you need in order to support your book? What kind of profitability is your book generating for your firm? Every producer should know, for example, exactly the moment of time when their book achieves a given threshold and they can blueprint for another account manager. These are key questions. This is the business side of it that a producer should master in order to successfully navigate their career.

There is clearly a big difference between sales and the business of sales. If you are attached to a team or an agency, they have a business to run, and learning that piece of it and catering to it—or, perhaps more accurately stated, conforming and integrating with it—will contribute to both your results and the prosperity you are seeking from your career.

The other critical piece to this phase of your career is understanding where your business has come from so far. What were the time wasters? What are the concentrations in your book? The three-to five-year period is the time to start evaluating this. I've seen producers portray themselves to me as a workers comp expert when only 8 percent of their book is composed of workers comp. Going back and looking at your book and examining your top three to five concentrations can be eye opening and will certainly help you grow your business. Looking at your history with those industries, you will hopefully see some successes that you can report within those verticals of your book of business. Ideally you will see repeatable themes and scalable themes that will help you achieve at least a million-dollar book of business.

It is important to understand what has the best chance of generating success for you: writing more cases or writing progressively larger pieces of business over time. In our view, from a practical application, those producers who tend to grow their books of business to be over a million dollars are all primarily focused on developing more expertise, more resources, and more capabilities that will enable them to write progressively larger cases of business throughout their career. That is the heart of organic growth. In the early phase of your career, you want as many cases and new business accounts as possible to build mass and a base. As you enter this and subsequent phases, you must now turn the corner and focus on writing fewer but larger accounts in specific niches to achieve a large book or you will peak early, as discussed previously.

Ask yourself how you found the business and what additional techniques for finding business you can now master. If you derive most of your business by cold calling or direct dialing or newsletters or cold canvassing, what other modalities or mechanisms of prospecting can you now master that will help move your book forward? Would it be learning how to do webinars? Would it be learning how to do podcasts? Would it be learning how to develop center-of-influence business? We don't want to be a one-trick pony. We want to master more than one methodology to attract and secure new business.

At this stage it's also a good idea to give love to your company and your team for seeing you through the first three years. Believe it or not, this period of time may have been as difficult for everyone around you at the office as it was on you. It takes a lot of faith and effort to deploy capital to somebody who's coming into this business. Once you survive, give some love to your team and leadership for supporting you through that first three-year phase.

Here are some questions to ask yourself in this phase:

- *Have I mastered weekly pipeline discipline?*
- *Have I performed a book audit, and do I understand its composition and where my business comes from?*
- *What am I doing to pursue progressively larger accounts?*
- *Who are the players in this industry, and what are they doing to win?*

Five to Ten Years

At this point your book of business is maturing, and you're moving upmarket. You can pay your way now, meaning you should be off a draw or a subsidized contract. You are beginning to pursue specialties, niches, and verticals. You are networking and beginning to obtain more introductions and referrals from the previous year's work. These characterize the common experiences of professionals in the five-to-ten-year increment.

Priorities

In this phase, specialization and pipeline discipline become critical, and time management becomes more important. Why? Because you've now generated a book of business, which needs to be attended to, and you're deploying more of your time to be a faithful custodian of their business. This will naturally take away from your time devoted to new business development. In other words, now that you've grown a book, attending to that book requires more of your time. Less and less time is available for new client generation, which means that learning time management and calendar discipline skills should now become a priority.

The ability to lead your support team is another important issue. One of the biggest factors in growing a book over half a million dollars of revenue and getting it to a million of revenue and beyond is how you work with your team. Instead of treating them, for example, as clerks, you want to treat them as account executives, empowering them and leading them. Fundamentally, the more you learn about how to lead a team at this phase in your career, the better off you will be long term throughout your career.

This is the time to master project management and delegation. Remember, you can delegate activity, but you can never delegate accountability. At the end of the day, you are accountable, but in order to continue to grow your book, you do need to delegate tasks and the execution of specific objectives.

At this point, expressing your knowledge, experience, and credentials to the world through social media and other channels becomes more important. This could happen on a blog, LinkedIn® professional networking services, or another modality. Think about it. You've been in the business a number of years now and you've seen, heard, and learned a lot. Now you can share that with the world, showcasing your work and discussing key issues that perhaps were either not attended to or overlooked by others in the brokerage community (which is why you most likely obtained the business you have in the first place). Besides white papers and social media, you could also provide content to an association that's dedicated to elements of your book of business: for example if you have contractor clients, a contractors' association. Associations are always looking for content that can serve their constituencies. Don't hesitate to explore these opportunities.

This time period marks the phase where you begin developing more center-of-influence business. This is possible because you now have a book of business. You can make trades with another service provider in exchange for referrals, and you have generated a solid client reference list to allow someone to feel comfortable providing an introduction and knowing you will handle it well.

This is also the phase to gain a better grasp on the business side—cash flows, revenue projections, and metrics. It's important to learn the difference between the insurance profession and the insurance industry. Let's use the medical profession to make the analogy. As an insurance professional who is concerned with new client generation and being a faithful custodian of their clients' business, you are similar to a doctor, someone who is actually healing a patient. In other words, you are both "client facing." That's the profession. Now, for example, in the doctor's case, the medical industry would be the individual running the actual hospital and making sure that staff is paid and profitable enough for new medical equipment to be purchased. In the best spirit of this, the industry should provide the resources, training, and capabilities for the professional to do their best work, though I recognize that this is not often the case.

However, in the purest and best spirit of this issue, the industry is responsible for running the business and the professional is responsible for healing the patient, if you will. So just as a medical professional must do the best job they possibly can to heal their patient, so the insurance professional must generate the best possible outcomes for their clients and be a faithful custodian of their business over time. The professional must recognize that they are embedded and connected to a business in order to do this work—be it for an agency or brokerage or an entity they themselves own. That business has specific needs, things that it needs to do in order to budget, forecast, pay staff, invest in new equipment, and so forth. The more that you can understand the industry side as a professional, the greater chance you have for success in rendering better outcomes to your clients as a professional. It's important for all of us to learn and engage in the business piece of it.

Here are some questions to ask yourself in this phase:

- *What specialties do I express to the world?*
- *Do I know my pipeline, my numbers, my metrics, and my cash flows?*
- *Do I understand the difference between sales and the business of sales?*
- *Am I developing myself as a leader for my team and others around me?*
- *Have I learned project management skills?*
- *Am I developing center-of-influence relationships within my local business community and through my top ten clients?*

Ten to Twenty-Five Years

At the point, the common feeling is that you see much of the industry and understand different roles and practice specialties. You receive far more introductions and cross-sell business due to your track record of success. Your community involvement is now paying off, and you're leading a team and contributing to colleagues within your agency.

Priorities

Establishing yourself as the go-to expert for given industries, verticals, and circumstances is key to this phase of your career. You want to be a thought leader and subject expert. In other words, you want to be published, even if that means publishing yourself on a blog, writing a magazine article, an association newsletter, or other publication read by potential buyers or others in your industry. Speak at industry events, association events, or even at peer groups your buyers have formed. It's also time to create a local business culture through an event, whether that is nonprofit advocacy, charity, or networking. Basically, you want to place your signature on the local business community's culture. You also want to write "the names" and other noteworthy accounts. "The names" is simply a term used in the industry for a highly recognizable firm, something anyone would recognize.

Position yourself as someone vital to high-level transactors, whether they are venture capitalists or private equity or other similar entities. You are looking for those who might be buying and selling firms and need somebody they can rely upon as a partner to vet any risks that are inherent with the firms they are considering acquiring. Those risks could be on the benefits side or property casualty side, or both, but they may have been missed in the initial vetting process by the acquirer and could make a material impact on the sale price of a given business.

Mastering center-of-influence development and strategic-alliance-partner development is key to this phase. You want to be an ambassador of your firm, your industry, and your profession.

Here are some questions to ask yourself in this phase:

- *Am I a go-to expert for given industries or specific transactions and circumstances?*
- *Have I published thought leadership?*
- *Have I spoken at events for the industry?*
- *What noteworthy and easily recognizable names accounts have I written so far?*
- *What percentage of my new business comes from center-of-influence relationships I've developed over the years?*
- *Have I created an annual event that places my signature on the local business community, or, at the minimum, do I contribute to one through my participation?*
- *What am I doing to become an ambassador for my firm and my profession?*

Twenty-Five Years Plus

By this time, you're a leader, whether you like that idea or not, and should be supporting and advocating for those 360 degrees around you constantly. Hopefully this includes sitting on industry boards and advisory committees and helping to develop the next generation rising within the industry. Your contributions to your agency and the profession overall will last many years past your retirement and you'll receive a great deal of satisfaction from those efforts, I assure you.

Priorities

Your priorities at this time are similar to those in the ten- to twenty-five-year phase: publishing, speaking events, leadership, service, writing the names and other noteworthy accounts, supporting local business culture, and social advocacy. This is the time for supporting your organization's overarching goals—perpetuation, mentorship, and succession plans—and achieving, for lack of a better term, professor emeritus status within your firm.

Here are some questions to ask yourself in this phase:

- *Have I been cited or quoted by industry magazines and journals?*
- *Have I been published by industry magazines and journals?*
- *Do I lead a fraternal or community organization, sit on a board, or organize an annual fundraiser event?*
- *What am I doing to support the overarching goals of my organization?*
- *What am I doing to help others get into the insurance business and support their development and success?*
- *What am I doing to help advance the profession?*

The career you want doesn't just happen; you have to be in the driver's seat. That said, any of us can get off track from time to time. We lose the way and need guidance to get back on the road. Be mindful of which career phase you're in, choose an appropriate priority to focus on, and take some steps to propel yourself forward.

Questions to Assess Career Navigation

- Am I trying or am I doing?
- What am I doing to become a dedicated student of my profession?
- Am I an individual contributor or am I a leader of a team?
- Do I fully understand my compensation plan?
- Do I know my buyer? Do I know where they go? Do I know what they read?

- Am I communicating openly and honestly, or am I employing sales tricks and pop psychology?
- Do I update my pipeline every week so I can track and measure the state of my insurance practice?
- Do I know my metrics, cash flows, and projections?
- Do I have the ability to budget, the ability to run projects?
- Am I focusing on the business of sales, or am I getting lost in the shuffle?
- Do I recognize that being able to find work is necessary to being able to do the work?
- Do I understand that my ability to promote and showcase my work to others is critical in today's environment and will be for many years to come?
- Am I the broker I would do business with? Am I the leader that I would follow?

CHAPTER 3

ANNUAL SALES PLANNING

Annual sales planning is not necessarily a popular concept. Just the idea can make people feel skeptical and trapped. Many people reject the idea of annual sales planning because they say there is no way look into a crystal ball and see into the future. Some producers are reluctant to lay out a plan and communicate it to leadership because they don't want their plan micromanaged throughout the year. It's also a common feeling among many producers that a lot of what happened the previous year in terms of sales occurred by happenstance or luck or "just being out there," which led to a sale. So how can they be expected to quantify that in a predictable and measurable business plan for the following year? While these feelings have a reasonable degree of validity based on certain circumstances, I plan to show you what makes sales planning a good idea and some practical ways to carry it out.

The Present *and* the Past

Many people think of annual sales planning as a strictly forward-looking enterprise, but I think the most valuable way to approach sales planning is to start by looking at the present and the past. Sales planning is a great opportunity to ask questions like these:

- What is the state of my insurance practice today?
- What happened in the twelve months leading up to this moment? What worked? What didn't work?

- What initiatives did I launch? Which ones gained the most traction? Which ones don't deserve more effort?

Forecasting is important, but the most productive course of action, in my view, is a rigorous examination of precisely where your business is today and what events have led up to its current state over the last twelve months.

There are a number of different methodologies that can be used for this. The first is process driven. This is essentially metrics by count and volume within phases of the sales methodology used—essentially activities and results. This is the classic methodology. When I started in the business almost thirty years ago, we used something called the 10:3:1 ratio—make ten calls, book three appointments, and close one sale.

The industry has changed quite a bit since then, and I'm not convinced that those ratios apply in today's environment for insurance practitioners and new business developers. Nevertheless, you could develop your own metrics—whether it's number of appointments per week or month, a certain number of introductions, or a certain number of mixers you attend each month where your buyers congregate. Whatever it may be, you want to establish these ratios in order to gain a clear lens into your business.

Here is one example of a metric you could establish. This is a pipeline tool that we deploy for all of our clients enrolled in our programs here at Rainmaker. If they don't have a CRM that they're regularly using, then we advise them to use this; if they do, then we ask them to use this as an adjacency since so many of these CRMs are geared more for reporting and forecasting for leadership than serving the actual needs of a given producer's new business development efforts.

A pipeline management tool that serves the producer recognizes and measures these stages:

- The preliminary phase is a staging area for leads and suspects.
- The research phase is for performing research and developing an approach.
- The discussion phase can be by phone or email, or even the first informal meet–and-greet appointment.

- The discovery phase (which is the beginning of what the industry views as a formal pipeline) is the fact-finding meeting with your prospect to talk about their concerns, issues, problems and pains, the current state of their business, and overall needs as well as the prospect's relationship with their current broker and what it would take to replace that broker. Also, there is the delivery by the prospect, perhaps in this phase as well, of materials that are required for quoting or for the review of policies, current rates, loss ratios, and other materials. This is what fundamentally defines the formal discovery phase.

- The capability phase is a meeting that communicates your capabilities, services, and resources as well as your process of managing a client's business over a period of either twelve, eighteen, or twenty-four months. This phase also includes a discussion of your team's credentials, a specimen project plan, and a list of prestige clients, testimonials, and so forth.

- The marketing phase is where you're actively marketing the account, including bid specs, negotiations, preparing spreadsheets, and the reporting of rate results. In some cases this phase may even include a meeting between underwriters and the prospect, with you moderating the discussion.

- The awaiting the decision phase is that period of time where you pace up and down the office, wringing your hands, and waiting for the green light. Many of us call this the dark period, and many brokers feel like all they do at this point is wait to hear from someone. But that is a mistake. We encourage all of our clients to manage the dark period aggressively: keeping in touch, asking if they have additional questions, making sure to know who the last broker is who's presenting and, if isn't you, asking for a debrief meeting before they make the final decision. Passing on information that corroborates the positions you've recommended, and even passing on existing client testimonials, are all contributory to this phase of the process. Managing the dark phase aggressively is a very effective way to generate more clients.

- Win or lose—This phase is basically the scorecard from your efforts.

Once you've established the ratios between the counts and volumes by stage, you now have a working model to establish reasonable goals. It is okay to pick one or two metrics to focus on. Developmental producers will tend to measure the beginning of this process—how many prospects am I researching? How many prospects am I booking a first meeting with? Veterans will tend to look toward the end of the pipeline. For example, many will feel like they're in a good position as long as they are awaiting a decision on at least three cases, or as long as they're giving five capability presentations per month. Sometimes they'll even go by volume, and toward the tail end of my career, I did this myself. As long as I had a certain amount of gross economic opportunity working through my pipeline and that volume was increasing month over month, I felt that my practice was healthy.

A clear assessment of your practice is key to the planning process. Sales planning isn't sales planning without this look at the past and present. Without a point of origin, how can you make it to your destination? Let's assume you want to drive to the Grand Canyon. Won't your route to the Grand Canyon be much different if you start in Los Angeles versus if you start in New York? It's great to identify a clear destination, but it's virtually impossible to identify the steps required to get there without a clear bead on the point of origin.

Assessing the Present

To assess the present state of your practice, there are many good options. A book analysis is a useful tool for identifying your point of origin. It's a perfect time to map out the renewal months for your accounts, and the size of those accounts. Ask yourself where your business is coming from. I've been fooled on this one a number of times throughout my production career. I had a handful of people that would send me a ton of business, but for whatever reason, I wasn't calling on them as often as I should have to continue developing the relationship. Perhaps I was taking it for granted—shame on me! But there were other people who I spent a lot of time with—people, as it turned out, who didn't provide or contribute anything back to the relationship. It happens; sometimes we err toward people we like to spend time with because they are fun to talk to, be with, play golf with, or go to social events with—yet from a business perspective that can be a total waste of time. It's something to keep an eye on, and it's a choice we all have to make.

So take a look at how well you know your top clients. Do you have a good relationship with them? What do you know about them personally and when was the last time you spoke with them? How often do you speak with them?

This is a good time to look at the smaller elements of your book and consider whether they serve your book of business and the growth of your practice or whether they are a drag on your progress. It's smart to look at these small accounts and apply a test. If they pass the test, keep them; if they do not, purge them. A reasonable test would ask the following questions:

- Do they have the opportunity to grow or are they static?
- Are they a good ambassador for your firm?
- Even though they're small, are they making introductions for you to more desirable pieces of business?
- Are they attached to the other side of the house where perhaps they represent a significant amount of revenue?
- Is this cross-sell business from a producer on the other side of the house that is essentially sending you small business now to see if you prove yourself before sending you larger pieces of business?

Remember that a key element to growing your book over time will be to increase the average size account in your book of business. It is a normal and healthy act to do a sweep of your book every year during the annual planning process to see if there are opportunities to purge small business from your book. By purge, I mean transferring fully to an account manager to run, sending it to an internal Small Business Unit (SBU) your firm has set up, or selling the block to one of many entities that purchase small account business and using that money to recapitalize your business and pursue larger accounts.

Annual sales planning is a good time to do a best practice analysis. What are you doing to win new business in the field and how does that compare with the top performers in your industry? Cash flow analyses and projections are important as well. How much are you writing each year, and if you keep writing at your current rate, where will you be in three, five, and seven years? Extrapolating your new business run rate and factoring in your attrition rate will give you a sense of where you'll end up in five years. Are you happy with that? If not, you need to make adjustments to increase your new business run rate to achieve your goals. You can't do annul sales planning without this information.

Looking Forward

Pick a start date for the year you're planning—whether it's the calendar year, fiscal year, your birthday, or the lunar solstice. It could be anything, but just pick a time to launch the plan. Dedicate the time to start planning, which can easily be done in two or three afternoons. If Friday afternoons are slow in your office, there you go! If you do catch-up work at home on a Saturday morning, there you go! There are 2,060 hours in what's viewed as the traditional work year. All we're really talking about is taking between four and six hours to plan so that you can have the most profitable and rewarding 2,060-hour year possible!

One easy way to do this is to look at your calendar and book from 2:00 to 4:00 p.m. on three Fridays in a row. That gives you six hours to develop and execute your annual sales plan. You might even finish early. It's not a big commitment in terms of time—especially given the 2,060-plus hours that you'll spend working in the coming year.

There are many ways to approach the year ahead. A qualitative approach tends to resonate highly with industry veterans. Those who have achieved a degree of proficiency in their activity levels, metrics, and appointments tend to structure their year (and their planning process), around achievements, accolades, and recognition. They might set the goal to be the number-one salesman at their firm or in the top 10 percent of producers within their firm. Or their goal might be to publish a white paper or be cited in an article in a newspaper. Developing a sales plan in harmony with these kinds of achievements is perfectly legitimate and popular among industry veterans and large book producers.

An initiative-driven approach is another common way to look at the issue. This essentially maps the pre-pipeline effort. Again, the formal pipeline that the industry recognizes begins at the first formal meeting and runs a course all the way to the end—whether you've won or lost the business. But the initiative-driven approach fundamentally focuses on pre-pipeline. It looks at what actions need to occur to obtain that formal first meeting. This kind of sales planning looks at adding activities that can help lead to that first formal appointment. Do you want to launch a webinar series next year? Do you want to do podcasts? Do you want to hold seminars or workshops? Do you want to do a brown bag lunch so clients and prospects can learn about new insurance trends that may benefit them?

You should have at least two to three sales initiatives running at all times. You don't want to be a one-trick pony. You want multiple channels through which people can do business with you. Suppose you strictly specialize in high-tech; high-tech has big ups and downs, leaving you vulnerable to what's happening in the market. Balancing your book with other industries protects you. Think of your book of business in the same way you might think of a mutual fund. You don't want just one stock. The purpose of a mutual fund is to invest in many stocks in order to spread your risk. It is the same with business development. We need at least two to three different channels or ways we can make money to grow our book, so that if one vertical dries up due to the state of that industry, we have additional ways to continue to grow our book with verticals in industries that are growing and prospering.

Focusing on key business drivers is another approach to sales planning. Those drivers could be new verticals, new territories, new programs, new capabilities, or new services. If an organization has launched a new program and wants it to scale, often they will select producers within the firm that they feel are able to drive it and gain traction at the strategic level for a given initiative. Obtaining a business driver initiative on your agenda for an upcoming year is actually a big compliment to a producer because the firm feels that you're able to drive it successfully, and they're putting that in your hands to do so.

Regardless of how you do your planning, I'd encourage you to run your plans by a colleague, partner, or advisor to gain input and suggestions. We all tend to go on wild goose chases from time to time. Or we want to be creative and pursue an aggressive initiative. Run your ideas by your colleagues to see if you're on track. Whether or not you follow their advice is another matter, but I think soliciting their opinion, so that you can obtain different perspectives on what you're doing and what you intend to do in the upcoming year, is valuable regardless.

Considerations as You Look Ahead—The Market, Your Clients, and the Competition

No matter what size agency you are with, reading the annual reports of the publicly traded brokers is a helpful annual practice. You don't have to read all two or three hundred pages. Really you just want to see how they describe their business. How do they perceive themselves? How do they believe they are positioned within the market? What capabilities are they rendering? Also take a look at the section that discusses threats to their business. Ultimately all of what you read will impact smaller firms in time and in varying degrees of severity, and this can be helpful information as you look toward the future.

Your annual sales planning process is a good time to look at competitor websites and join the company pages they've set up on various business networking sites. Why? Because throughout the year, you'll obtain information on whether they've had layoffs, they're adding new people, or they're starting a new division or expanding into new territory. All of this information can be handy in terms of your ability to re-engage prospects that might have those brokers or exploit a material agent of change that has occurred in that relationship between the incumbent and the client.

Use online auto-notifications and LinkedIn® professional networking services company pages to monitor your top clients and your top competitors. Refreshing these each year during your annual sales planning process will help you stay abreast of everything you need to know as you are hustling for new business during the course of the year and are busy juggling lots of activities and projects.

Annual sales planning is a reminder to consider your idea of an ideal client. Throughout our careers, the definition of an ideal client should change. When we start out, we have that anything-and-everything methodology of writing business through our relationships, no matter what industry they're in.

As our book grows, and we get more into mid-market, we start to establish different verticals and our definition of an ideal client will continue to evolve. The point is that to grow an insurance practice sustainably over time requires us to write progressively larger pieces of business while we continue to shuffle off the smaller elements of our book. Therefore, we need to continually adjust the definition of an ideal client upwards if the average size account in our book of business is going to increase over time.

This is the time to look at the narrative of challenges you faced in the previous year. What happened? What were the issues? You also want to identify any training or resources required. Don't ever stop sharpening the saw. By continuing to develop yourself as a professional, you will be able to achieve greater and greater outcomes for your practice.

Sales planning isn't about seeing into the future, but it is about making your future happen. You cannot possibly reach your destination without knowing where you want to go and charting a course to get there. Having a plan does not mean you'll never get off track or you won't have flexibility. It does mean you'll be able to recognize when you're off track and make the necessary course corrections.

Questions to Assess Annual Sales Planning

- Have I established a clear picture of the state of my insurance practice?
- Do I understand what has transpired in the last twelve months—how I obtained new business and what happened with any clients that I lost?
- Do I understand my cash flows?
- Do I have a plan to do sweeps of my book of business to identify any account rounding or any cross-selling opportunities?
- Am I applying a test to my smallest accounts to see which ones I should keep and which ones I should divest from my book?

- Are there any business driver initiatives I can volunteer for that are important to my firm?
- What achievements do I wish to have this year? Have I submitted a plan to leadership so that they can understand what I wish to accomplish so they can lend support?

CHAPTER 4

CALENDAR DISCIPLINE

The need for better time management is a critical issue raised by our clients at Rainmaker again and again. We have found that the traditional view of time management certainly can help people make progress, but there is another approach that in our view trumps that and can provide more effective results. In this chapter we'll examine the traditional view of time management compared to accounting for seasons in your year, the key times to plan, the best time to build initiatives, and the times we are required to do heavy renewal work, which all have various concentrations throughout the year.

Time management isn't just a rigid set of principles. It's also about knowing the tendencies of your buyers and knowing how you like to work. Do you like to take care of all of your administrative work in the morning and then chase business in the afternoon? How do you come out of a weekend? Are you raring to go on Monday, or do you need a couple of extra cups of coffee on Mondays and to delay most of your client-facing work until the following day?

We're also going to talk about the concept of "enabling structure." When I was coming up in the business, I avoided structure because I felt like I needed to flex and flow to meet any given demand at any given time in order to secure new business from prospects or to attend to the needs of an existing client. I also felt that lack of structure enabled me to respond to client emergencies quickly and immediately. Down the road, when I began to add structure, I discovered that structure actually gave me more time to do so!

It seems counterintuitive that setting up your calendar with standing meetings or standard and repeating times to attend to certain activities would actually give you more time to do other things, but I think you'll find as I did that it really does. It sounds confining, but it actually is not. Of course we'll talk about using technology to manage your calendar as well as how to compartmentalize and identify different days of the week to apply specific effort. Ultimately I believe strongly that you'll find all of this will benefit your new business development activities and top line growth for your practice.

In our consulting work here at Rainmaker, we have found that the producers who have come to us utterly immersed in chaos often have very sparse meetings on their calendar. When we start working with producers on compartmentalizing days and dedicating certain times for activities that will support their career above and beyond simply booking prospecting, final presentations, and client renewals, they tend to advance their careers significantly. None of us does this perfectly, but perfection isn't necessary. Don't think of calendar discipline as scheduling every minute of every day of your week; I encourage you to start out with trying to master how you begin the first four hours of your week and how you end the last four hours of your week. If each day of a five-day work week represents 20 percent of the total week, by mastering eight hours of your week, that means you're 20 percent ahead!

Time management actually has very little to do with how you manage your time. It is really about working more efficiently and mastering the understanding of the difference between fixed (or recurring) meetings versus variable meetings as well as the sequencing of events. When possible, your actions should serve various elements of your career, not just one. For instance, consider the software programs that help you build a great presentation. The time spent in learning that skill serves many areas: It will serve your ability to make a capability presentation. It will serve your ability to present ideas to your team and to leadership. It will serve your ability to do webinars and podcasts. That's an example of deploying one unit of your time to serve your practice and your ability to grow your book over time in many different areas versus learning something that only has one immediate and direct application. That's what time management is really about.

Calendar discipline can also support your leadership of your team. If you have account management available to you through a pool or direct assignment, then, make no mistake, you are no longer an individual contributor; you are a leader with the corresponding responsibilities. One of those responsibilities is to provide consistency and predictable habits and preferences your team can support. Calendar discipline will have arguably the most impact with supporting that issue. If your team knows your schedule, what days you like to do certain things, when there are standing meetings with you, what to bring to those meetings, and so forth, it helps people follow you and contribute to your efforts. But if you are immersed in chaos with no structure, then your team may stand back and wait for you to tell them something specifically, because they don't know exactly what to do or how to contribute. Support from your team (and organization, for that matter) cannot be rendered to you unless you provide a consistent structure. Period. No one can follow a random chaotic z-particle crashing this way and that; it doesn't work that way.

Applying Key Drivers to Calendar Discipline

The first step to developing a realistic management of your time is to identify the key drivers of your success as an insurance professional navigating your career. What do you need to attend to? What do you need to assign dedicated time to? One example of a key driver is dedicated prospect time. Best practice is to have at least eight hours a week of dedicated new business development time. We recommend using four days and two-hour blocks of time. It could look something like Monday afternoon from 1 to 3, Tuesday morning from 8 to 10, Wednesday afternoon from 2 to 4, Thursday morning from 7 to 9. The value of a structure like that is the variance. Also, by leaving Friday unused, you have the option to use that as a spill day. You might need that if something crops up during your usual allotted prospecting time that requires you to defer it forward to a Friday, for example. That's what Fridays are for!

I understand that setting a schedule like that may give you some anxiety. People often fear that things will crop up exactly during the scheduled times. And indeed, that might happen. That's why a spill day is useful.

A common pitfall that we all experience is that we spend a lot of time and effort to develop a piece of business and finally when the flag drops and they say, "Yeah, we can meet with you at this time to wrap this up," then we just clear everything off our schedule to do it. But a key time management technique is to simply say something like this: "I can meet with you then, but I'd have to move something. I have this other time open, however. What do you want to do?" People will often agree to the other time. Think about it this way: If half the people agree to that alternative time, you now have more calendar integrity, because 50 percent of the time, that dedicated prospecting time isn't being moved. But if we don't even bother to ask the question, then 100 percent of the time our calendar will be disrupted.

When you're scheduling your prospecting time, I would encourage you not to simply put in a two-hour block that says "prospecting." Label it by different prospecting methodologies that are working for you. Tuesday could be cold calling. The next day could be networking through social media platforms. The next day could even be taking a prospect to play golf. The next day could be cold canvassing. Also, there will be some variance naturally by month or even by quarter. Maybe you're going to do a quarterly brown bag lunch, or a speaking event, or a monthly webinar. The idea is to vary it, put it on your calendar, and be specific: cold canvas ten businesses; ask my top ten clients for introductions; have lunch with a client and ask them for three introductions.

Another key driver is working with your team. I think probably one of the biggest time management pluses that I've had in my career is having a weekly standing meeting with my team. I used to be one of those brokers that would check in throughout the day: "How are you doing? Do you need anything? What's going on with this? That? The other thing?" I wasted a lot of time, and an older veteran coached me and said, "Look, meet with them every Wednesday." Wednesday works because it's in the middle of the week, meaning you don't have to worry about long weekends interrupting the schedule. And, of course, that meeting should have a set agenda. That way your team knows what you want to discuss and will come prepared. That's time management.

Consider this: If you are not meeting with your team once a week and you don't have a set agenda, you're going to have a lot of chaos.

That one meeting can actually free up a lot of time. Consider too that a weekly meeting on a Wednesday means that you're never statistically more than two-and-a-half business days away from any crisis that could lead to jeopardizing either a client or a prospect if left unattended. Frankly, there's nothing that you can't get fixed within two-and-a-half days if you jump on it.

Working with leadership is another key driver for your career. Do you have any regular one-on-one coaching set up? Are you required to update or track your business plan for the year on a quarterly basis? Any recurring meetings or sales meetings? All of this belongs on your calendar.

Attending to what I call "business government issues" belongs on your calendar as well. Do you have some dedicated time to checking your commission reports? Whenever you're paid, look at the cycle of being paid and how much time you need prior to that to scrub your commission report so it's in time for your next paycheck. Whatever the time period is, put that on your calendar. That's an issue of sequence. What you don't want is to look at your commission report, be surprised, do a commission scrub, find money, and then wait two weeks or a month for the money. That's inefficient.

Professional development is another key driver that belongs on your calendar. This is really learning more about transactional excellence, studying for and obtaining professional designations, going to industry workshops and events, and even listening to podcasts. Put it on your calendar.

Lastly, promoting your work is an often neglected key driver. Schedule time for working on blog posts, articles, podcasts, speaking events, and webinars. How are you revealing your work to the outside world? This is critical for business development and for your own growth.

Calendar Discipline and Buyer Tendencies

Remember that buyers represent groups of internal and external stakeholders whose needs and roles must be defined, as well as their schedules. When do they arrive at work? When do they leave? Do they work on weekends? Can you call them on a weekend or after hours? How much travel do they have, and how can you reach them when they are traveling? Do you have the cell phone numbers of at least your top ten buyers? If they are traveling, can you send them a text? Some buyers work on internal matters exclusively during certain periods of the day. In other words, some reserve working with external vendors in the afternoon, and internal stakeholders in the morning. Or, sometimes they'll do it by specific days of the week. This is why we encourage producers to vary their new business development times throughout the week. Some buyers may only be accessible during the morning, others might only be accessible in the afternoon, and some may like you to message them during the hours before and after the standard workday.

It's also important to know your clients' budget season. Do they have fast times, slow times? When do they do their strategic planning? There's a big difference between how private and public firms operate. Many privately held firms do calendar years. Some corporations might choose a fiscal year, and certainly many, if not all, public companies do so. When do they do quarterly reports and annual reports? When do they do monthly earnings calls? Get a sense of their responsibilities and busy times. As a very simple example, can you even imagine if you were trying to write a CPA firm and you called to ask them for a meeting on April 15th?

Knowing when your clients and prospects budget and forecast for the following fiscal or calendar year can be a great help to you. The larger the firm that you are working with, the more people who are looking at the budget. You may have a primary buyer, but they have internal stakeholders they need to please in that process; if you learn what that process is and what the stakeholders surrounding your buyer within that organization want, you can better support your primary buyer and come out a winner.

It also helps to put on your calendar the little things that can go a long way to developing a strong relationship with clients: birthdays, anniversaries, and even important community or charity events they are involved with. Even if you can't attend, you can let them know you're making a donation. These sorts of thoughtful gestures can go a long way to developing a solid relationship over time.

Calendar Discipline and Your Work Preferences

Understanding and recognizing your own work habits, tendencies, and preferences, and incorporating them into your schedule will serve you well over time, so structure your calendar in accordance with the way you like to work. Are you a hard charger in the morning? Do you like to do client backend work in the morning, and chase business in the afternoon? Structure your calendar accordingly. Do you have more energy in the beginning of the week than the end? Some people start their week strong and like it to be a little softer and easier at the end. Others like to make Friday their strongest day because they feel like most of the industry doesn't do much on Friday, so if that's their busiest day, they're actually getting ahead of the competition. Schedule it in a way that makes sense for you.

Do you like to schedule your field days? I've noticed a lot of senior executives in the industry schedule their travel for Tuesday through Thursday. That gives them four days, Friday through Monday, at home. Again, think about your travel on a strategic level.

When do you like to update your pipeline and attend to other business matters? Friday afternoons? Saturday mornings? I know a lot of people with families who choose to work one late night a week and, for whatever reason, they tend to pick a Monday night.

As you set up your calendar, it may help you to think in terms of each day meaning something. I think the most productive people tend to compartmentalize their days. What do Mondays mean for you? Are they an admin day? Is that your sales meeting day? What is it? What does Tuesday mean? Is this a dedicated day for you to launch sales initiatives and outbound activities aligned toward new business generation? Are Wednesdays and Thursdays dedicated to client-facing work? Are you out in the field these days? Is Friday about working with underwriters and your team, updating your pipeline, laying activities out for the following week?

It is your choice how to structure your schedule, but if you're doing all parts of your job every day, that is a mistake. Everyone needs time to focus—chunks of a few hours dedicated to specific activities. This will enable you to get up to speed and catch a rhythm, which ultimately leads to greater productivity. Each day should mean something, so structure your calendar accordingly.

Let's further discuss this concept of enabling structure. It is a fairly difficult concept to articulate, but I do believe it's important and can make a big contribution to your overall success. Think of it as a guitar string. If the string is too tight, it will snap. If it's too loose, it won't play. Think of your schedule this way, and tune that guitar string to make the most sense for you. If you do not have, for example, any standing meetings or dedicated time on your calendar to pursuing key business drivers, you'll find yourself immersed in chaos, with little chance of advancing your practice. If you have too many standing meetings and your week's structure is too demanding, you will not be able to flex to client emergencies and attend to what can sometimes be immediate demands issued by prospects in the courtship process. No one can strike the perfect balance, but pay attention to whether you are sensing chaos or feeling unable to respond effectively to random and immediate requests and adjust accordingly.

In my view, the traditional definition of task lists is seldom effective for most insurance creatures. From my experience, what works is deploying our efforts within given increments of time. Compartmentalizing at least two-hour increments of time for given duties tends to be the most effective. What group of tasks lends itself to a weekly dedication? What group of tasks lends itself to a monthly recurring dedication? What tasks lends themselves to quarterly and yearly? Put it all on the calendar and watch what happens.

Using Technology
Your calendar is one of the most effective business tools that you have at your disposal. Learn how to set up recurring meetings, invite others, embed links to webinars, send invitations, attach documents to review before the meetings, and determine who on your team is available at given times.

Most CRMs have a feature that will sort schedules and identify when a group of people can meet. This beats sending an endless stream of emails to coordinate schedules in order to identify when you can set up a capability presentation or a discovery meeting. I have seen transactions derailed by the email threads sent by brokers trying to coordinate a meeting with a prospect. It can leave a team looking disorganized and incapable. If you don't know how to do this, ask your IT person immediately. Most CRMs have this feature, and I'd encourage you to master it.

I've also found that an effective tool is simply sending a meeting invite for a proposed teleconference. Include the day and time as well as the discussion agenda on the meeting description. This is a good way to move forward when you're trading emails or simply not connecting via phone. Send the invitation and then follow up with an email saying, " I know we've been having trouble connecting. I just sent you a meeting invite. I'm not trying to be presumptuous about your schedule, but I'm just trying to keep things moving. If the time works for you, please feel free to accept it. If there's another time, please propose that."

Remember, time management doesn't have to be perfect. It just has to be more effective. I encourage you to improve your ability to manage time. If you improve the management of your time by just 20 percent, that's a lot less chaos and a lot more time available for new business development, which will advance the growth of your practice. Start with the bookends of your week. Control the first four hours of how you begin your week, and control the four hours of how you end it. Start there.

Questions to Assess Calendar Discipline

- Do I understand the seasons of the year for at least my top ten clients?
- Do I understand the work habits and preferred methods of communication for at least my top ten clients' purchasing officers?
- Am I using calendar technology to make scheduling easier and more efficient?

- What standing meetings do I have as recurring meetings on my calendar?
- Do I have dedicated time on my calendar for focusing on the key drivers and activities necessary for growing my practice?

SECTION 2: GROWING YOUR TOPLINE REVENUES

CHAPTER 5

FILLING YOUR PIPELINE

We all face times when we've exhausted our pipeline. Any of us who have been in new business development for any reasonable period of time know that. Sometimes we become so busy working cases though the pipeline we neglect to generate new prospects, and if those cases fall through then things come up empty for a bit. It happens. In this chapter we'll put this event in its proper perspective and examine how to work your way back to a full pipeline.

Perspective

It is perfectly natural to have peaks and troughs in a given sales cycle. Fundamentally, when we look at this as a cycle, the closing process actually is the indicator that we're coming upon a peak of production. Once we arrive at the peak of production, closing ends, which defines the production peak. In other words, the production peak has three milestones: when closing begins, the actual peak, and when closing ends—meaning we have successfully dispensed of the activity in our pipeline to either a sale or no sale. Now begins the trough. The trough begins when opening new cases for the next cycle commences, and the bottom of the trough follows that. As we come out of the trough, opening ends and now we're successfully working those opportunities through our active pipeline, back to what we hope will be a peak. That defines the overall process and cycle of sales.

Production troughs are naturally longer than production peaks because it takes less time to close a transaction than to nurture and develop one. Courtship can take a year, or even two or three. But actively engaging and closing a transaction might be just four or five weeks. That's why the peaks are shorter than the troughs.

If you want to shorten the production trough, you have to start the new cycle closer to the peak of the previous cycle. Shortening the trough can mean significant increases to new business generation each year. The peaks will take care of themselves. You can't eliminate a trough, but you can mitigate it by shortening its lifetime.

Troughs and peaks become more severe over time as a book grows and commonly occurring renewals and expiration dates accumulate naturally on different focal points of the year. For example, those in the employee benefit industry have very heavy renewal cycles on January 1; in fact, statistically somewhere between 38 and 42 percent of their clients renew on this date. There is not much that can be done about that. Ultimately any producer will write business whenever they can, regardless of whether or not it continues to increase the severity of their peaks at certain times of the year. Peaks are going to occur, but the issue is how to make your time during the troughs as productive as possible and shorten that cycle whenever feasible.

Techniques for Mitigating a Sales Trough

A book analysis is one important technique for mitigating sales troughs, and at Rainmaker, we recommend to our clients that this be done yearly. It will help you understand the demands upon your time each year as you attend to client renewals. A book analysis will give you a sense of the rise and fall of available prospecting time that you have available to you throughout the year. This will help you to see when to launch sales initiatives, when to pursue professional designations, and when to take vacations. It will clearly reveal to you the times of the year to develop and introduce additional resources, as well as the best time to take on internal projects, education, and workshops that you want to conduct.

Calendar discipline is very important. Set up all your recurring meetings in advance throughout the year—whether they're internal, client renewal cycles, midyear client reviews for your top ten clients, or even one-on-ones with your account management team. You should also set up your Q1, Q2, Q3, and Q4 projects, your workshops, the build out of new resources and capabilities, and the upcoming month's available prospecting time.

We have found from practical experience in working with clients that setting up weekly prospecting activities can be challenging due to the peaks and valleys of client-related activities that interfere. Rather than saying you need to book two appointments a week, which equals eight per month, we feel that loosening that up from a weekly metric to a monthly metric is more practical and easier to sustain.

It is, however, important to generate a weekly cadence in terms of when you're in the office, when you're doing fieldwork, when you're handling administrative tasks, and so forth. These activity metrics do lend themselves to a weekly cadence.

For your top ten clients, we highly encourage setting up yearly service calendars. These should be twelve-month calendars that delineate when the marketing cycle occurs. The calendar should address client advocacy, compliance checks, and introducing new capabilities, along with specifics regarding who on your team or theirs will perform these tasks as well as, of course, when they will be completed.

Doing this for your top ten clients will generate more free time for you throughout the year. Your time with your largest clients will be spent more efficiently and you will eliminate a lot of noise. Think of it like a road map to understanding what will happen over the next twelve months. You could use service calendars for all of your clients, but simply having it for your top ten will eliminate a lot of chaos and give you a lot more room to prospect for new business and retain your top ten since they will tend to make up more than 50 percent of your annual revenue.

Another benefit is that this saves you a lot of time in scheduling. It is perfectly normal upon acquiring a new piece of business to create a standing schedule to address semi-annual, quarterly, and monthly meetings with them. Setting up the meetings well in advance is favorable to both parties—for the client, for the insurance producer, and for the teams to whom they are both attached at their respective organizations.

We also recommend setting up a prospecting hierarchy. Most of us try to allocate at least eight hours a week for new business development, but given emergencies with clients and issues that crop up, it's virtually impossible to maintain an eight hour a week cadence dedicated to prospecting efforts. For that reason, it's wise to identify which efforts are critical to make in a given week. What are your priorities? If you only have time for three out of ten things you normally do to develop new business and manage your practice, which will you do? What gives you the biggest bang for your buck in terms of growing your book of business?

Filling Up the Pipeline

Most pipelines are designed to record events in a process that begin with the first appointment. Managing a pre-pipeline is the key to filling it. In other words, managing the steps that lead up to a formal discovery meeting is what will ultimately fill the pipeline. The traditional measurement or definition of the beginning of a pipeline is the first meeting. At Rainmaker we reject that. We feel that the real issue is how to fill a pipeline. What steps lead up to that first substantive formal meeting?

Most likely that first step is research of some sort, which probably begins with simply downloading information in line with your firm's sweet spot. Whether your sweet spot is cargo or high-tech firms with under 100 employees, you first have to find them. Then the real research begins.

Identify the firm's history and the culture of their company and read all of their most recent press releases and any financials you can access. Basically you are hunting for information that will allow you to cobble together an approach with enough specificity that the prospect will be interested in a first meeting. That defines the pre-pipeline and that's how we fill it. Most producers who are struggling to fill an empty pipeline are really focusing on the first meeting. Without quantifying pre-pipeline events, most producers tend to forget about roughly a third of the actual opportunities available to them. Most producers do not have an action plan for more than 50 percent of their pre-pipeline activity. Clearly the issue is not so much the pipeline itself. We encourage focusing on the steps and measuring the steps that lead up to that first meeting. That's how you fill a pipeline effectively.

Practical Tips

Here are a few practical tips to use as food for thought:

1. Ask for introductions, not referrals. Asking for referrals has a connotation of responsibility and accountability by the referring agent. It's risky and not necessarily convenient. Asking for introductions is easy, convenient, and low risk. There is no implied fiduciary responsibility, so they are easier to obtain. Here is a proposed action item for you. Identify your top ten clients on LinkedIn® professional networking services and then search their connections for their counterparts at other firms. Research those companies and then ask your clients if it's okay with them if you introduce yourself to those individuals. You'll often hear, "Of course you can."

2. Perform a search. You can search firms by location, industry size, purchasing officer, and many other attributes. For each result you'll be able to see who you know that is a first degree connection to the purchasing officer. You're trying to identify anyone you can obtain an introduction from. Here's an action item: perform a search by size and purchasing officer title—whether it's the vice president of HR, director of HR, or CFO. Determine who you know that's connected to that individual and ask for an introduction. Then reach out to them, mention your common relationship, and ask them for ten minutes to introduce yourself.

3. Cultivate center-of-influence development. CPAs, lawyers, and business consultants are easy to find and understand the value of mutual trades. They often have clients with situations that require an insurance broker, and it can be a very fast sales cycle once an introduction is facilitated. Center-of-influence development can be pursued by typing your address into a search engine and doing a search of nearby CPAs, lawyers, and so forth. You'll get a nice map with many pushpins designating whoever you're searching for. At that point it's easy to review the websites of those firms to determine whether they have practice specialties that are in line with yours. Are they holding workshops you can contribute content to? Can you speak at one of their luncheons with clients? These can be very good relationships. You can draw a lot of water out of these wells, and if you have a somewhat sizable book of business, you are very attractive to them in terms of doing trades; so at the very minimum, they should be open to a discussion with you.

Introducing yourself and seeing if you can bolt onto their distribution channel can be a very worthwhile effort. Here's an action item: Conduct an online search for local law firms, CPA firms, and CFO outsourcing services, and review their websites for common industries served, workshops they host, their client list, and their professionals. Doing research prior to the approach is critical. Then set up a time to meet to learn about each other's businesses, and discuss trades. You can also ask your top ten clients what CPA firm and law firm they use, and ask if you can introduce yourself. The introduction is quite simple, all you need to say is, "I wanted to introduce myself since we have a client in common. Do you have some time to chat?" They have an obligation frankly to have a conversation with you because you have a client in common. Where it will lead is up to you and your ability to explore that opportunity, but gaining access should be easy for you. Expanding your relationship network through your clients' vendors is simple and effective.

4. Use research to add specificity of approach. Remember, researching a prospect is easy and it takes just a few minutes. What you will learn will help you package your approach to mention certain items that will have more of an impact than a general, or canned, approach. Research will always improve your chances of securing a discussion or even a first meeting by orders of magnitude.

Here's another action item: Stage twenty-five companies in the preliminary category of your pipeline. Perform online research on each to learn more about the company. Use LinkedIn® professional networking services to see if you know somebody in common with the purchasing officer you're targeting to have a conversation with. Then you can send messages citing specifics and ask for a discussion.

Here are some lessons to remember: Sales troughs and empty pipelines are normal. Because they are normal (and to be expected), you should be prepared to plan, mitigate, and manage this event. Managing the pre-pipeline is *the* way to do that and to refill the pipeline. Identifying companies, researching them, approaching them with a degree of specificity, and sequencing your messages to convey your credibility, knowledge, and experience will enable you to differentiate yourself from others and earn their attention for a substantive first meeting.

Peaks and troughs are a given for anyone engaged in new business development. It's better to understand the cycle and work with it than to fight it. Know your own peaks and troughs and the factors that play into them. Working diligently on the pre-pipeline is the most efficient way to level the cycle and weather the troughs.

Questions to Assess the Pipeline

- Have I done a book analysis and determined my fast and slow times of the year so I can manage my efforts accordingly?
- What am I doing to identify companies, research them, and approach them for an initial discussion, be it formal or informal?
- Between the initial discussion and the formal discovery meeting, what do I do to promote my work and nurture the prospect until they're ready to meet with me?
- Am I using LinkedIn® professional networking services to identify second-degree connections that can help me obtain introductions in order to engage a new prospect in a discussion?

CHAPTER 6

GENERATING FIRST APPOINTMENTS

W hat drives success when it comes to generating that first appointment? Where does that level of engagement come from? When you are prospecting, first and foremost keep in mind *where* you are prospecting. Are you prospecting for situations that are head-to-head, even playing ground against competitors? Or are you focusing your efforts on your competitors' weak areas or soft spots? It is worthwhile to look for areas where there is an "imperfection of fit" because it can increase your chances of not only obtaining that substantial first meeting, but also winning the client. In this chapter we'll take a look at prospecting methods, but in particular we will look at the value in taking a multilayered approach.

Prospecting Methods

In a Rainmaker Advisory poll conducted in 2014 we received data back from 1,114 retail insurance brokers across the country of all practice specialties to rank their prospecting effectiveness by different methodologies. They ranked them as follows in terms of efficacy:

- Introductions and referrals
- Networking
- Strategic alliance marketing
- Affinity group marketing
- Direct calling or cold calling

- Social events
- Webinars
- LinkedIn® professional networking services and Facebook
- Seminar selling
- Business mixers

Ultimately, to generate the highest probability of success as an insurance practitioner in terms of getting a substantive first meeting with a prospect, you need to be good at more than one method of prospecting. Why? Because people who may not ordinarily be accessible by cold calling can be accessible by attending a business mixer or a charity event. Also, many people who are not accessible by a phone call can be very accessible by email or through messaging via LinkedIn® professional networking services. Learning at least three to five prospecting methodologies and mastering them provides a much better chance of expanding your reach and connecting with potential buyers than using just one.

Let's define the difference between cold calling and direct dialing. No research goes into cold calling. It is a general and canned approach. In other words, the same approach is used regardless of who you're talking to, the size of their business, and their tenure in their current position. Cold calling is really about the prospect hearing about your body of work for the first time. There is no relationship connection or familiarity, which will naturally breed some degree of skepticism or, as some people call it, buyer anxiety.

Cold calling doesn't use special timing. It ignores the biorhythm of the year. It's not effective to call an account that renews in December in the month of May, because they are not concerned with the renewal cycle. With no precision in terms of timing and timeliness of the call and without knowledge of a material change in status, a cold call is merely an outbound reach to a given prospect that inherently will have marginal efficacy.

Some studies have suggested that with cold calling approximately 2.8 percent of appointments are made on the first contact, 3.1 percent of appointments are made on the second contact, 5.3 percent of appointments are made on the third contact, and 9.6 percent of appointments are made on the fourth contact. Finally, 78.2 percent of appointments are made between the fifth and the twelfth contact. These statistics show

how challenging cold calling can be if it is being used as a singular modality for obtaining a substantive first discussion with a potential prospect.

Direct dialing is best described as a call made after some degree of research, allowing some specificity of approach. In other words, on a direct dial call, you might indicate that you're aware that the prospect's renewal is on an upcoming date, which is fairly imminent, or that their mod factor has increased significantly, or the carrier they're with has had a downgrade in their financials, or their reported loss ratios are high, which could result in a significant rate increase. Any material agent of change that you find through your efforts and research allows you to present a more specific message and differentiate yourself.

In 2014, 1,114 producers respond to a Rainmaker advisory poll in which we asked, "How many hours are available to you for prospecting every week?" A significant number indicated that they have fewer than two hours a week for prospecting. More than 40 percent indicated they only have three to five hours. Here's what this means. If you're confining your prospecting efforts exclusively to cold calling, you will achieve perhaps four to six low-quality prospect meetings per month given the time that you have available. Considering the limited time most of us have available for prospecting, it makes sense to find and master the most productive ways of prospecting.

Questions that Concern a Prospect

There are many key questions that must be answered in the prospect's mind for them to engage in a substantive and productive first appointment. Understanding these questions can provide you with a helpful benchmark. You want your prospecting methods to answer these questions in the prospect's mind:

- Who is this person?
- Do we know anyone in common?
- How did they come to us?
- Are they a credible professional?
- What is their work history?
- What are their work products?

- Is there a searchable history of their work?
- Have they published anything?
- Have they had successes with people like us?
- Are there any skeletons in the closet?

In this day and age when somebody can use the Internet to find out quite a bit about any of us within a matter of minutes, it's important to be able to answer these questions.

A Multilayered Approach

Here is an example of a multilayered approach and appointment-setting strategy. (Of course, this will vary by tenure classification, but this paints the picture.) A good place to start is targeting introductions from first-degree connections via LinkedIn® professional networking services. Look for those that fall within the right parameters for you, and introduce yourself through those existing relationships.

The next step could be rounding from your existing client base. Following that could be speaker or content events, such as speaking at a lunch-and-learn event that you host at your office or at a law firm or bank—wherever you can provide content to an audience of potential buyers. Next could be local events and business mixers where buyers congregate. Identifying and attending those can really help to build your career. Ask your key clients what events they attend and whether you can go too and buy a ticket for you both. The idea is to go where they go so you can network with their counterparts. Last up is direct dialing to increase the X dates that you have in your inventory and hopefully build new relationships locally over time.

Over time you will discern what combination of prospecting efforts yields the best results for you. But it's important to have at least three to five different methodologies, or "tracks," in order to succeed. This will help you resonate with more buyers, thereby increasing your pool of opportunity. It will also add resiliency to your client base, increasing your overall retention rate. Just remember, how you prospect will generate the kind of client you have. If you're just cold calling with a pitch about saving money, you're going to generate a lot of rate-shopper clients. It takes more research, specificity of approach, and sequencing of messages to convey your credibility, knowledge, and experience to differentiate yourself from others and earn attention for a substantive first meeting than ever before.

Be sure to align your prospecting methods to suit the three basic communication types and buyers: prestige buyers, logic-and-fact buyers, and emotional buyers. This messaging will vary. Typically, the CEO or other organization leader will be interested in prestige buying and want to know what other firms their size or larger you insure. They'll be curious about any awards you've received, what you've published, and your client list. Logic-and-fact buyers, such as the CFO, are more driven by case studies and metrics. Emotional buyers may often reside within the HR stratum. Just always keep in mind who you're talking to. There is always so much you could share with a potential buyer about what you can do for them, yet you are given very little time to do so in the initial approach in order gain their attention and secure the first substantive appointment. The key is to consider your specific audience and their role within the firm so you can align your messaging in a way that has the highest chance of striking a chord that will resonate with them.

First Appointment Characteristics

In the old school of thought, these appointments were fundamentally a live meeting, typically one to two hours in duration. With Main Street business, it would be a meeting with one highly empowered buyer. In a mid-market business these meetings often include a multi-stakeholder presence. It can be difficult to get more than one person around the table, and it can be a political risk for the person who has been your initial contact and is organizing everyone to get them to the meeting. It requires significant commitment on the part of the buyer in marshaling all the internal stakeholders into one meeting to listen to you. It also requires a degree of preparation on the part of the buyer, which is fundamentally high risk and low convenience for them. Requesting an initial meeting that is a substantive "all hands on deck" fact-finding session tends to be a more effective approach down market. In other words, it works better for Main Street business than mid-market.

For mid-market business, a first appointment could be a teleconference, an informal meeting (internal or external), a webinar demo, an exchange on LinkedIn® professional networking services, or even the exchanges of text messages. These typically take fifteen to forty-five minutes. Multi-stakeholder presence is much easier to arrange vis-à-vis a teleconference or a webinar demo than getting everyone in the same meeting room. Think about it. In a mid-market business, leadership and key stakeholders might be spread out over a number of different offices and they may only gather in one office together a few times a year. A teleconference where they can call in remotely is much easier to arrange than a formal live meeting where a number of the internal stakeholders need to travel and reconcile all of their schedules in order to accommodate the meeting.

This requires a low degree of commitment and zero preparation on the part of the buyer and is fairly easy to schedule (and even reschedule if necessary). It's low risk, and it's convenient. The meeting and/or process should provide some value irrespective of them moving forward with you in a formal marketing or even BOR process. This could be vis-à-vis an opportunity analysis or a discovery analysis, an assessment providing some degree of guidance as to a potential next step. This is certainly a more effective approach for mid-market and large market business.

When you look at your prospecting methodology, you need to consider the risk-to-convenience factor. At the top of the pyramid is high risk and low convenience, and at the bottom of the pyramid is low risk and high convenience. Where does your initial approach for a first appointment really fall here? Consider how risky and how inconvenient the initial step is for the buyer. If it's too much and you are not getting the number of first appointments you desire, consider watering down the nature of the first meeting you are requesting so that it is more convenient and less risky for the other party to engage you.

In terms of the pyramid, the bottom could be LinkedIn® professional networking services, forums, a brief chat, a text, an IM—all convenient and low-risk modalities of first engagement. Next up on the pyramid could be email and links to recorded demos or work exhibits. Next could be a teleconference, an informal meeting, or live webinar demonstration, all of which represent incrementally more risk and less convenience. Then moving up further on the pyramid, an assessment or diagnostic process; at the top, a live formal meeting representing the most risk and least convenience.

If you are having challenges generating a substantive first live meeting, ask yourself whether you are making it easy, convenient, and low risk. Consider some ways that you might be able to create some softer steps to that first formal live meeting.

We also know that prospecting efficacy tends to vary by tenure classification. For example, for those in their first three years, cold calling and direct dialing are foundations. Attending business mixers, adding connections via LinkedIn® professional networking services, networking, and cold canvassing are also important. These tend to be the most effective prospecting methodologies for those in the first three years.

Those in the three-year to ten-year increment have accumulated a number of expiration dates and renewal dates from activities in the first three years, so they are able to direct dial. This tends to be productive when you know their carrier and perhaps some gripes about their relationship with their broker. Of course, business mixers, networking (including online networking), and affinity group marketing remain important during this time. It's also the time when you start to align your efforts around the higher concentrations of industries within your book in order to develop a vertical and a niche.

In the ten- to twenty-five-year tenure classification, introduction and referrals tend to be the predominant modality of prospecting. Networking, strategic alliance marketing, affinity groups, webinars, podcasts, and social media outlets are also part of the picture. The twenty-five-year-plus time frame is much the same.

All of this reveals that as you pass through different tenure classifications, you will change the way you prospect. This knowledge helps us to navigate our careers over time, but it also helps sales leaders to understand that somebody starting out in the business cannot generate outcomes using the same prospecting modalities that an industry veteran can.

———

Effective prospecting answers the many key questions in a prospect's mind. Who are you? Are you credible? Who do you know? Those are just a few of the questions in the front of your prospects' minds. In the information age, ensuring that those answers can easily be found on the Internet is an important way to help yourself win business. So what will they find when they perform a search for both you and your firm? Using a multilayered approach to reach out to prospects and develop your relationships easily and conveniently is the most surefire way to make it to a first appointment.

Questions to Assess Prospecting and Generating First Appointments

- Is there an "imperfection of fit" that I can solve?
- What size businesses am I directing my prospecting efforts toward?
- Is that in line with my market segment?
- Am I prospecting within my firm's sweet spot?
- Are the brokers that currently hold the prospects I'm approaching from a firm smaller than mine or the same size or larger, and how do I shape my approach accordingly?
- How much time am I dedicating each week for new business development?
- What is my courtship process leading up to the first substantive new appointment with the prospect?
- How often have I researched a prospect and identified someone I know in common through LinkedIn® professional networking services to approach the prospect for an appointment?

CHAPTER 7

RESEARCH—THE RUNNING START

A "running start" is everything. Research clearly demonstrates you are a professional, and it differentiates you during the approach, increasing your chances of securing a meeting. It also helps you shape your discovery questions, allowing you to not only obtain better information, but increasing the prospect's value assignment toward you as a viable alternative to the incumbent broker. Research differentiates you from others competing for the same business, and it apprises you of material events during the courtship process that may contribute to adjustments and/or emphasizing different aspects of your value proposition to increase your chances of securing the business. Research is fast becoming the price of admission for successfully courting and winning mid-market and large market business.

By the way, I'm not talking about locking yourself in a room for two weeks and reading annual reports, 10Ks, and all of that. We live in the age of the Internet, and it's very easy to search a firm or an individual and gain valuable information. This not only allows you to approach a given prospect with some specificity, but it allows you to ask more impactful and insightful questions once you obtain a first meeting.

Research Across the Sales Process

Understanding the various types of research will help us in our discussion. There are three types: applied versus basic, exploratory versus confirmatory, quantitative versus qualitative.

Applied research is designed to solve a basic problem. Basic research is designed to understand the underlying principles of a problem. The second type of research is exploratory versus confirmatory. Exploratory research is research into the unknown. Confirmatory research is used when a theory exists and the objective is to see if the facts are there to support the theory. Lastly, there is quantitative versus qualitative research. Quantitative uses polls, surveys, and so forth to measure variables against numeric scales or benchmarks. Qualitative studies are based on direct observation of human behavior through interviews or by reading transcripts, blogs, or other posts by the individual being researched.

Let's talk about the application of research across the sales process—pre-approach; approach; discovery meeting, capability presentation, and marketing results; and then of course the actual stewardship phase with the client. In the pre-approach, exploratory versus confirmatory is the desired trajectory, and that information can be obtained online from various sources.

The theme behind the approach phase sounds like this: "Based on our preliminary research, we suspect we can help you, and we'd like to discuss what we've found in order to see if indeed that is the case." You could support that by embedding links in your outbound email to them requesting a meeting. Other possibilities are attaching a PDF of a white paper or article or even inviting them to join you on LinkedIn® professional networking services as a connection so that they can review your credentials and your work history.

In the next phase—the discovery meeting, capability presentation, and delivering the marketing results—you're weaving what you have found through your research into questions and emphasizing capabilities that flow logically from their responses to the research you've done for maximum impact. This could be application of practice-specific tools such as Advisen or FreeErisa, looking at mod factors, or even just setting up online auto-notifications for news about the target account and the competitors who are vying for the same piece of business.

Once you are their broker of record, research can help by monitoring agents of change and competitor development. In other words, you want to use online auto-notifications to monitor news about the broker that you replaced because they may be attempting to come back and regain the business. You want to get a good sense of what the competitor you have displaced is doing in the market as well as other brokers who you beat out in this process. Check their company websites periodically to see if they've added any new gadgets, capabilities, resources, or expansions that might threaten your ability to maintain the client that you just won.

A Stronger Approach

The value of research is clearly demonstrated in the way it strengthens the approach. If you were to approach someone without doing any research, it might sound like this:

> Dear Mary,
>
> I'd like to introduce myself. My name is Joe Broker at ABC Insurance. We specialize in helping employers lower their insurance costs and I was hoping to discuss your programs with you. Would you have some time available either Monday at 2:00 p.m. or Tuesday at 10:00 a.m.? I eagerly wait your response.

Here is an approach that can be constructed after fewer than ten minutes of Internet research:

> Dear Mary,
>
> I recently came across an interview your CEO did for the local business journal where he was discussing your company's plan for growth and the importance of managing operating expenses. I did some additional research on your company and believe we may be able to help you serve those goals.
>
> I also noticed from LinkedIn® professional networking services that we both know Jane Doe, who speaks very highly of you by the way and encouraged me to reach out to you. I'm attaching a testimonial from a client who had similar goals as a demonstration of our work, along with some information about my

company and professional background. I'd like to request a brief discussion to see if indeed we might be of service to you and your company. Would you have some time later this week or the following? Please be kind enough to let me know a time that suits your schedule.

These are two very different outbound messages, both designed to compel a first face-to-face discussion. The message constructed without research is weak and nonspecific to the recipient. The one done with research is specific and impactful. If you had time only to engage one broker, which one would you engage? Most people would certainly select the one who did some research and comes to the conversation with some degree of understanding their circumstances.

Sources

There are almost endless helpful websites to help you find what you're looking for. Start, of course. Don't forget to look at trade blogs, forum posts, press releases, white papers, WorldatWork, and CFO Magazine. Also, ask your clients what they read to stay sharp and keep informed. You'll find some great publications that way. Anything that your buyer reads, you should be reading as a broker because that helps you understand the buyer's mind, the trends they're monitoring, and the language and terms they use and are most familiar with in their respective industries.

Keep in mind that the process of research is not a background check. Avoid services that offer phone trace and personal data for sale. You are not looking for that kind of information. You are looking for agents of change, awards, product releases that have been praised (which may signal growth), acquisitions, capital infusions, new leadership, a new purchasing officer, or a new boss for the purchasing officer. You are also looking for any commonality of relationships or experience—whether it's military service, education, common charities that you support, and so forth. In short, agents of change combined with some element of relationship connectivity will yield the greatest chance of obtaining that first meeting. Build your connections on LinkedIn® professional networking services. One hundred connections is where the magic starts happening in terms of finding second degree connections, with 500 as a reasonable goal over time that will yield the best results for you.

Ideally you want to have information come to you so you don't have to chase it. I encourage you to join forums on LinkedIn® professional networking services. Look at your top ten purchasing officers and see what groups they've joined. Join those groups because you'll automatically be notified of any update or content, and anything someone has published within that group that is being shared with, and potentially read by, one of your customers or target prospects.

You can also set up online auto-notifications for your top ten clients, perhaps some of your larger prospects, some key competitors, and maybe even some carriers. This is a great way to monitor human capital. This will be a source of information about any material agents that have changed or new information in any of those categories, which will allow you to jump on things quickly.

I also encourage signing up for your competitor's email list. On many of your competitors' sites, there will be a free subscription form you can populate. They'll send you their e-newsletter and send you information and updates about their firm. It's okay to sign up. Use your real email. If they deny you, fine, but if they accept you, which will happen the majority of the time, you'll be getting information about your competitors locally. At the same time, your clients may be getting their free e-newsletters and announcements as well as the prospects you are both are pursuing, so it's a good thing to know about whatever they are sending out to them so you can be prepared.

Competitive Intelligence

First and foremost, I encourage you to use caution with competitive intelligence. Often times, word of mouth and gossip are tainted goods. It's only a worthwhile lead if you can find third-party data about the matter from a credible source—whether that's the brokerage's website, a press release, an earnings report, or published news from a credible source. Be cautious about consumer blog posts and message board posts from dissatisfied customers. Sentiments expressed should be ubiquitous and not one-off gripes.

If you choose to use such information, I encourage you to be sterile about the delivery and make no value assignment toward the data. Here's an example: "Our research team came across this, and I thought I would bring it to your attention. If this is a concern to you, I would encourage you to discuss it with your broker." Basically you want to let them know you found something that might have an impact on them and they might want to discuss this with their broker. Then step away. That is a much more powerful and professional approach than running around muckraking or casting aspersions on the incumbent broker based on a piece of information you found, which may not be completely accurate. Competitor information is a slippery slope, so be very sterile about the delivery of it.

Information is a powerful tool. Research is what allows you to obtain that powerful tool and use it effectively to catch prospects' attention and win their business.

Questions to Assess Your Research Usage

- What am I doing to build my connections on LinkedIn® professional networking services? Do I have a weekly or monthly goal? How will I get to 500 connections?
- What forums have I joined where my purchasing officers congregate and share ideas?
- Have I set up online auto-notifications for my prospects, top ten clients, competitors, and my own firm?
- Am I monitoring the movement of human capital? Have I set up saved searches on LinkedIn® professional networking services, so I'm constantly getting information about people new to positions that I can reach out to?

- Have I signed up for my competitors' email lists?
- Am I careful about using competitor information?
- Am I always coming to the table with a running start?

CHAPTER 8

THOUGHT LEADERSHIP AND SELF-PROMOTION

After you have been in the industry a while, you have the opportunity to win more business by promoting the work you've already done. This is a great method for winning new business, but it doesn't happen on its own. Experience is wonderful, but if you don't communicate that experience and the success you've generated for those who have done business with you to your potential clients, then it won't do you any good.

In this chapter we will discuss some ways to develop your own thought leadership and content. You want to promote what you know and get it out there for others to see, which will hopefully support any transactions already underway and help you engage and penetrate new accounts and clients.

Buyers don't live in our world. As insurance professionals, we can easily recognize what makes a good insurance broker, but it is more difficult for our buyers because they are not in our industry. If they take a look at Broker A and Broker B, what do they see? How do they really know who's a good broker and who is not? Suppose a prospect looks at Broker A and sees a sparse profile on LinkedIn® professional networking service—no testimonials, no prestige client list, no blog postings, and no thought leadership. Broker A has never been quoted in the trades, makes no commentary on any insurance forums, and doesn't have any white papers. The prospect can't see much at all, so Broker A is a bit of a mystery.

Broker B has a strong profile on LinkedIn® professional networking services, complete with testimonials and recommendations, a prestigious client list, and a blog. Broker B is quoted in the trades, has searchable commentaries on forums, community involvement, and case studies and/or white papers that they've issued.

Broker B appears highly credible because there is a searchable evidence of their work. Of course it is possible that Broker A is better than Broker B, but there is no evidence of that, and buyers want evidence. Think in terms of how people make decisions and what could happen if a purchasing officer makes a mistake in changing brokers. It could impact their career negatively or even lead to their outright dismissal. Having a body of evidence to demonstrate your work is critical to lowering buyer anxiety and moving the process forward.

Do You Promote Yourself?

One of the questions we ask in our annual survey is, "Tell us how you use PR and media relations to increase your presence, promote yourself within your local business community, and distinguish yourself from the competition." Here are some of the responses we have received:

- "I have not utilized media very much throughout my career. I've been interviewed by the local news station and quoted a couple of times only."
- "I write a safety column for an association newsletter; I would like to do more of this."
- "None of the above. I'm involved in several community organizations, which makes me most visible at this time."
- "I'm not actively doing that but I would like to engage more. I enjoy being involved in the community and have had PR opportunities with presentations to donors at local nonprofits."

As these responses reveal, we get so focused on doing our work that we forget to promote it or position it with potential buyers. Apparently we have a lot to learn about packaging ourselves as insurance professionals.

Much of what this comes down to is being a thought leader, and the benefits that come from that. According to Wikipedia, "A thought leader can refer to an individual or firm that is recognized as an authority in a specialized field and his expertise sought and often rewarded." The Oxford English Dictionary says this phrase originated in 1887 so it's been around a while. Thought leadership is often used as a way of increasing or creating demand for a product or service. For example, high-tech firms often publish white papers with analyses of the economic benefits of their products as a form of marketing. That is a part of the high-tech culture, but it needs to become more a part of our culture as brokers.

Nuts and Bolts of Self-Promotion

Sometimes a simple lack of knowledge of the practical step-by-step process of how to do something stands in our way of doing new things. If thinking in terms of issuing thought leadership and publishing a white paper or blog post seems overwhelming to you, understand that anything you publish should have a title, subtitle, your byline, the content, and then a brief bio. You can even use a formula to help you organize and narrow down your content. Your first white papers or blog posts could follow this simple, three-step formula: a mistake, the damage caused, and the remedy.

In terms of application and use, you could send an email attachment to a prospect as you're trying to get in the door and in the email say, "By the way, I know you've got a lot of people contacting you asking if they can talk to you about your insurance program, but I just thought I would share with you an exhibit of my recent work which I think you might find interesting." This differentiates your approach, which will yield better results than simply hammering a prospect for a first meeting.

You don't have to limit yourself to sending these to prospects. White papers, case studies, and articles can also help you develop center-of-influence business. Send them to a center of influence while you're courting them to do trades or asking them to introduce you to some of their clients. This will help you prove your expertise and it can go a long way toward ameliorating any anxiety they might have about making introductions.

You can also send your content to magazines or trade newsletters. What associations govern your key verticals or industries? Those associations are often starved for content and looking for something credible to publish for their constituency. Identifying these associations and offering content to them creates tremendous exposure for an insurance professional to scale within an industry where they already have a foothold with some clients.

Bolstering Your Profile on LinkedIn® Professional Networking Services

LinkedIn® professional networking services is like a business card on steroids, and it's another opportunity to make your expertise known. Take a look at your profile there. Does it express your value proposition? Are you expressing thought leadership? Do you have recommendations and testimonials? You want to give it everything you can, because the majority of people you reach out to will look you up on LinkedIn® professional networking services before giving you any response. They will want to know if you are a credible professional to connect to for a substantive change in their insurance programs.

If you were going to meet a potential client for the first time, would you wear professional attire or hiking gear? Mastering online networking is just another way to present yourself to the world and make a good impression.

Differentiating Yourself with Thought Leadership

One of the most important ways to do this is by providing valuable content that demonstrates your knowledge and experience. If that sounds overwhelming, think of it this way: Choose a topic and identify the top five mistakes that are made by brokers in any given area of transacting insurance. Outline the damage caused by each mistake as well as the remedy or solution to it. For example, you could identify the top five mistakes brokers make in managing their clients' renewal process, or the top five most overlooked policy exclusions for the oil and gas industry or the top five mistakes brokers make in managing the open enrollment process.

If you lack confidence in your writing skills, you have a lot of options. Dictation and transcription might be a great choice for you. There's a site called Upwork.com where you can dictate content and somebody will transcribe it. Then you can simply clean up the draft and it will be ready to publish. Of course there are also copywriters who will do the writing for you, or copyeditors who will clean up whatever you've written. A few hours of your time and a few hundred dollars to a copywriter or copyeditor will provide you with a great return downstream over time because you'll be able to use it over and over again either directly or by reference for many years.

———

Presenting yourself as an expert in your field may sound intimidating, but it doesn't have to be. The idea is simple: Get the knowledge in your head out into the world with a format that can be easily digested by others and share it with audiences who can benefit from it!

Questions for Assessing Self-Promotion

- What will a prospect find if they decide to check me out online?
- What materials and resources am I providing to the internal advocates who are helping me secure their company's business that will help them justify the decision to move forward with me to the other stakeholders in the decision-making process?
- How often am I checking my online presence?
- Am I updating my profile on LinkedIn® professional networking services with recommendations and testimonials as I receive them?
- What "thought leadership" have I recently constructed and distributed?

- Am I identifying publications or other distributions of "thought leadership" where I can publish content to reach potential clients?
- Have I identified resources that can help me with creating and editing content?

CHAPTER 9

SALES AND THE ASSIGNMENT OF VALUE

Assignment of value answers the "so what?" question. It is really the essence of sales from my perspective and experience. When we sell, we are assigning value, letting prospects know how our service will serve them, what exactly it will do for them, and how it will help them meet their goals. As business developers it's easy for us to focus on nuts and bolts—features, products, price, and the credentials of our company. In doing so, we tend to forget to enable the assignment of value—what exactly we can do to serve our clients in terms of helping them achieve their desired outcome. That's what it's really all about for any vendor or service provider—having your presence ensure the achievement of your client's desired outcomes!

This chapter is going to examine the merit of classic communication skills, but not pop psychology–based trickery or general sales theory offered up in the newest shiny box. Instead we'll discuss demonstration of concept, stakeholder tendencies, and assignment of value toward the insurance broker. We'll have a summary of points to consider and incorporate into your practice as well as some questions to ask yourself along the way.

The Philosophy of Communication

The ancient Greeks were the first to examine the philosophy behind communication, and they broke it down into three pieces: ethos, logos, and pathos. These were established as the root form from which all communication flows. Many popular and heavily marketed sales training methodologies rely heavily upon attempting to understand human psychology and use that understanding to manipulate an outcome. This is, by the way, a very imperfect and highly complex science that is difficult to execute and, in my opinion, comes with serious ethical implications. After all, do you like the idea of being manipulated by someone? Then why learn methods designed to do so with others?

What you'll tend to find with pop psychology–driven sales methodologies is that they amount to nothing more than tricks, tips, and manipulation; most buyers sense that and (once they do) withdraw. At the end of the day nothing in my view beats open and honest communication. An open and honest exchange will get you further than anything else. Rather than attempting to become, for lack of a better term, a silver-tongued sales devil, which some people out there think is a good thing, what will truly help you is furthering your skills in communication. You want to become a more effective communicator rather than trying to manipulate someone's psychology in line with what you're trying to sell them.

When I started my career there was a lot of this pop psychology–based sales theory running around. But human beings are complex creatures and understanding whether they're an ENTJ or a driver analytic or an expressive driver was a bit confusing to me to say the least; and, it was difficult to assess and shape communication on the fly to line up with those assessments during an exchange. Frankly, it felt like a puzzle to me, and, ultimately, I abandoned this philosophy of sales because I just didn't like talking with fellow human beings this way! Based on my experience, it's madness to think that these methods of trickery, persuasion, and pop psychology can be implemented on the fly, in real time, during an exchange with anyone. How can anyone execute that effectively? In my opinion, nothing beats respect, etiquette, and open and honest communication. Having performed in the top 3 percent of every sales team I've been a part of during my career in the insurance industry, I can tell you the aforementioned attributes of respect, etiquette, and open and honest communication are indeed what get things done. The higher up you go and the larger accounts you write, I promise you the conversations will become extremely direct, and everyone at the table will be more than smart enough to sniff out a cheesy salesman using trickery and dismiss such individuals quickly.

When I learned this concept of ethos, logos, and pathos, it helped me greatly because it was easy to remember and apply, and it provided an honest way to interact with others. I found it to be an effective, and, frankly, somewhat eternal concept that lends itself to constant modernization of application as well as to adaptation to the age and background of the audience. It has helped me a lot, so I share it with you here.

Ethos is a mode of communication that applies to the ethereal; in sales it is an attempt to communicate one's value proposition on the basis of the seller's character, credibility, and elements of prestige, whether assigned directly to their work, their team, or their firm, or even by recognizing the stature of those who have already awarded their business to you. Pathos is a mode of communication that appeals to a given listener's emotions. You'll see this a lot with financial service professionals, especially life insurance professionals. However, for business-to-business insurance transactors in the mid-market to large market segments (that's you—the focus audience for this book), you may find pathos communicators concentrated within human resources, and to a lesser degree with others no matter what their role. Logos is an appeal to logic. It relies on empirical data and persuasion by reason, empirical data, case studies, ROI analysis, and so forth.

Let me give you a sense of this concept. We train the producers that we work with how to sell a spoon for ten thousand dollars. I know that sounds absurd (and it is) but it gets their attention! How would you derive that much money from selling just an ordinary spoon? We teach them to use the communication forms of ethos, pathos, and logos; to do so illustrates and reinforces the concept by demonstrating their practical application.

Would you buy a spoon for ten thousand dollars?

Most of us would say of course not. For an ethos buyer the trajectory might be, "Hey, this spoon was blessed by the Pope" or "This spoon was used by Henry VIII" or "This spoon was used by Muhammad Ali to eat his Wheaties before every fight that he won." What are we doing? We're enabling the assignment of value toward the spoon along the channel of ethos—prestige and credibility.

A pathos trajectory of communication would be emotion and relationship driven. Here are some examples of enabling the assignment of value through a pathos trajectory of communication: "Makes me feel like a million bucks when I eat from this spoon." "It gives me confidence and peace of mind." "Reminds me of the home I grew up in." "Makes me feel powerful, like I can do anything." "Gives me a sense of history and connection with others."

The logos trajectory is logical and empirical. "It was forged from a rare combination of metals, which has never been reproduced and will never bend or get scuff marks." "Master craftsmen made this spoon by hand." "It's a prototype and the only one like it on Earth." "It was made over two thousand years ago." "It has been documented as one of the rarest spoons in the world." "Spoon Manufacturers Association of America has rated this the best spoon ever made."

In general, a buyer at the CEO level is an ethos buyer. Credibility is important to them. What clients do you have on your prestige client list that they might recognize and respect? Who are you connected to that they respect? Those at the CFO level tend to make decisions by logic, empirical data, solutions, and testimonials—numbers, numbers, numbers. Those from HR may likely be swayed by pathos. They're asking questions like these: "How do you know so and so?" "How did you come to meet with me?" "How are you connected to my networks—the people that I care about?" "How will you take care of the members of my client group?" "How will you help them when they experience distress that can impact their work here?"

It won't fall in line perfectly every single time, but if you start to look at the issue and examine how various people communicate, you will see ethos, logos, and pathos. This enables you to shape your messaging to resonate with each stakeholder at the highest level.

In terms of opening strategies, typically there is time for only three elements of messaging in a call or an introduction. By combining or using each method (ethos, logos, and pathos) sequentially, you'll have the best chance of hitting a chord with your prospect. Once you hit that chord, then you can keep your communication consistent with that method. The initial moment of engagement should incorporate all three because you can't assume a particular method will always appeal to a particular role or job title. Once you determine which channel resonates, then you can align the subsequent messaging of your services accordingly.

Here are a few examples: "How do you feel about your broker's effectiveness in supporting your role as CFO for XY Industries?" This is a pathos approach. "How effective has your broker been in managing your costs and assisting you with financial projections for your budgeting process?" That's a logos approach. "How well is your current broker equipped to support your firm's growth and strategic objectives?" That's an ethos approach. Think about it like fishing: you're going to fish with an egg, a worm, and a lure, and based on whatever the fish are biting that day, you're going to re-bait and re-string the other poles with the bait they happen to be biting on that day!

Assignment of Value toward the Broker

On Main Street, and even up to lower mid-market, it's common to see consumers view an insurance broker as someone who wants to sell them something. Additionally, many just look at a broker as someone who simply provides them with rates each year and handles a claim problem when it arises.

Where do we want to go? What's the desired outcome? What we want is their assignment of value toward our ability to keep their plans competitive, provide them with different strategies, and share best practices of what others do to successfully mitigate and control costs. This applies to everyone. And as you move upmarket, you'll often find that virtually everyone you talk to wants to work with somebody who makes them look good to their boss! Enter the politics associated with sales!

Toward the end of my career I worked with a larger account that revealed a great deal of political sensitivity among the internal stakeholders. I learned to adjust to this and to be very clear: If I do my job right, you're going to look fantastic to your boss. I will generate wins and successes for you. That resonated with a lot of people. If you are portraying yourself as a success generator and creating successes that your primary buyer can hold up to their leadership, it clearly makes them look better—and it serves you. You are not only generating success for your primary buyer, but also for their constituents, and for the people they work with 360 degrees around them, which a great way to do business. In the best relationships, the buyer sees their broker as someone who is always thinking two steps ahead—someone with a strategic vision who is looking out for them, helping them succeed, and ensuring their desired outcomes are being achieved and illuminated to others with whom they work.

People tend to focus on four steps to enable the assignment of value:

1. What is it?
2. What does it do?
3. How is it applied?
4. What will it do for me?

Those four steps are a good start, but to enable the assignment of value we need to go one step further: What larger purpose does this serve? *That* enables the assignment of value. Understanding the type of preferred communication method embraced by the person you are speaking to will help you enable the assignment of value. It's not so much what you can do for them. It's what your services mean to them. What it can mean to them is getting a raise, receiving a bonus, keeping their job, or looking great at what they do to their boss. That has value, and that's important. Right, wrong, or indifferent, those elements specifically as well as those associated with them play into people's decision-making process—so don't forget to address them explicitly in your exchanges with your buyers!

————

Answering the question "so what?" is the producer's job. What can your services do for your prospects and clients? Understanding communication styles and preferences will help you communicate that value to your prospects in a way that resonates with them and will ultimately help you grow your book.

Questions to Assess Assignment of Value

- What am I doing to master the three basic forms of communication?
- Does my initial approach incorporate the three basic forms?
- Upon receiving feedback from individuals I approach, do I see how they communicate and then align the messaging of my services to their preferred form of communication?
- Do I enable the assignment of value for all the services I offer?
- How do I use ethos, logos, and pathos for my prospecting and marketing communications?
- What do my services mean to my prospects specifically, both for their succeeding in their roles as well as for helping them achieve their enterprise's goals and objectives?

CHAPTER 10

DEVELOPING CENTER-OF-INFLUENCE AND STRATEGIC-ALLIANCE-PARTNER RELATIONSHIPS

This chapter is focused on developing center-of-influence business and strategic-alliance-partner relationships. Mastering this area of your insurance practice will catapult your book forward by orders of magnitude. The fundamental principle behind this is that you can sell more *through* people than you can *to* people. We're going to examine the difference between center-of-influence and strategic-alliance partners, how to identify and approach good center-of-influence and strategic-alliance-partner business, and how to structure the relationships and develop them to their full potential.

In the annual poll we conduct here at Rainmaker, one of the questions we ask is: "What percentage of your new business comes from center-of-influence relationships that are external to your firm and you've developed yourself?" and 25 percent of respondents indicated that they get more than half of their new business from center-of-influence relationships. By the way, most of the respondents to that component of our poll were multimillion-dollar book producers. I believe that speaks to the significance of this issue as you continue to grow your book of business sustainably over time. Let's face facts: You have less and less time available for new business development efforts as your practice matures. Therefore, your new business development efforts must become more efficient and most likely rely upon center-of-influence business development in order to continue to grow. The poll also indicated that 34 percent of respondents get less than 5 percent of their new business from these relationships, and another 31 percent derive only 5 to 20 percent of their new business efforts this way. Clearly there's a lot of work to be done here by many.

The Differences between Center-of-influence and Strategic-Alliance-Partner Business

Let's begin with some definitions. A center-of-influence relationship is an individual contributor who is highly influential and respected in the business community. It could be a sole proprietor in the Main Street business segment who has influence with other small business owners in the community. It could be a sole proprietor in a profession that holds the business you desire, such as a CPA or lawyer or business consultant, or even an individual within a large enterprise who has many counterparts.

A strategic-alliance-partner relationship takes place at the enterprise-to-enterprise level. It's usually an enterprise with which you can cross-pollinate business without an overlap in services. It *could* be an enterprise where there is an overlap of services; when that occurs, it is important to have covenants about non-compete and poaching to protect your arrangement with them. It could also be an enterprise with which you can co-market to each other's mutual benefit and cross-pollinate business referrals with no conflict up and down through its professional hierarchies and tenure classes. This obviously would be an ideal situation.

Three Drivers of These Relationships

There are three drivers behind developing center-of-influence and strategic-alliance-partner business. The primary driver is that it compresses buyer anxiety. When you are working through center-of-influence channels, you are essentially leveraging the relationship and bypassing the prospect's buyer anxiety and confusion about who you are. This allows you to engage more quickly in an open and substantive exchange about what they need and what you can provide to them.

The secondary driver is it allows you to tap an inventory of business held by another professional—one who has already established a channel to your desired buyer. It's like bolting onto a distribution channel that is already established by another vendor to your primary buyer. Lastly, and as a tertiary driver, this enables the development of new business passively while you're engaged in actively seeking new business. It essentially allows you to duplicate yourself. In this way, over time the apples will fall from the tree right into your lap as you are "plowing the field" by actively pursuing new business with your primary new business development efforts and methodologies. Center-of-influence initiatives are not meant to operate in lieu of active new business generation directed to a target prospect. They are meant to augment—not replace!

Characteristics of Center of Influence

This type of business tends to consist of highly controlled transactions with fast sales cycles. Typically, when this occurs, there's an active referral from a center of influence to one of their clients that you can write insurance to, and usually there's a crisis that was expressed to the center of influence by their client, requiring that the given situation be addressed very quickly by you. Short of that, these relationships may often begin almost as tryouts with the bottom-tier business of their own portfolio clients; that way there is little risk to them if something goes wrong. It's important to give this business 100 percent effort and generate success. After that, you can weave in messages regarding what you're really looking for. Remember that it takes some time for any professional to trust you with their key accounts.

A common mistake occurs here among many producers. They work hard to develop a center-of-influence relationship and the first few cases are small, unprofitable, and have a lot of challenges and or expense associated with them in order to successfully address their circumstances. A common mistake is to say, "I'm not interested in working on this type of small and difficult case." Fundamentally, what the center of influence is doing is giving you a trial, a kind of a test period. It's perfectly logical for anyone who has a client base not to trust someone else with one their top clients because if something goes wrong, the last thing they want is to have one of their most significant pieces of business jeopardized by a referral to another vendor. So it is common for them to try you out on small, perhaps unprofitable, and challenging cases. The big mistake producers make is avoiding or rebuffing these initial referrals from a center of influence, which results in them rarely receiving one again.

The way to win is to accept all of the initial referrals, thank them, work hard on them, do the best you can, and report back to the referring entity about what you were able to do. At that point you can reinforce what kind of business you're really looking for. If you were unable to help the referral, you could report back with something like this: "We were not able to help them, but it appears that they just need to work through a current situation and upon doing so, we invited them to reach out to us. We're happy to help them after the issue has been successfully dealt with. They appreciated our advice and agreed to do so."

Think of this kind of business development like a water spigot. When you open up a water spigot, only a few drops come out at first. The mistake is cranking the handle back the other way and saying, "Gee! If there's only a few drops, I don't even want to try any longer." The right way to do it is to open up the spigot, allow a few drops to come out, open it up again for more drops, then open it up again and see that now it's starting to flow. This is how center-of-influence business often develops. It can take a year and a half to up to three years until you have enough history established as a credible resource for them to trust you with their larger accounts. This is perfectly normal and to be expected.

Practical Steps for Building Relationships

In rare cases, sometimes a center of influence will offer you their account list en masse in exchange of course for yours as well. This can happen when people really hit it off with one another. This is a mistake. The best approach from my experience is to obtain three to five introductions at any given time. That's an easy number to contact, approach, and have discussions with. Then you can get back to the referring agent and say, "Here's what happened with these referrals. It went well. Can you introduce me to more of your clients that are in this specific industry or that specific industry?"

By asking for just a few referrals at a time, you're creating the ability to have a relationship with that referring agent over a long period of time. The communication you have during that time strengthens your relationship and will give them more visibility into your work. This will allow them to identify more opportunities within their portfolio of clients that you can contact, which over time will become more and more ideal for your practice.

There are some logical steps for identifying and approaching center-of-influence and strategic-alliance-partner business. The first is to look at your book. When you look at your book, you really have three layers: the smallest, the middle, and then your largest clients. There's a subtle issue operating here. Some people like to choose what I call the "meaty middle" of their book—not too small and not too big. Then you ask those clients who their CPA, their banker, and their law firm are and whether they would introduce you to these individuals. Here is one way to do it: "I wanted to introduce myself as we have a client in common. We're looking to establish relationships with whom we can partner to trade business. Would you have some time next week to meet and discuss one another's businesses to see if there might be a potential alignment between our firms?"

There's no way to know ahead of time where the conversation will go, but potentially opening these discussions could allow you to obtain access to these individuals who hold portfolios of business, elements of which can be very desirable to you as an insurance professional. This is an easy access channel. What happens from there is up to your ability to demonstrate your value proposition, how you can support them, how you can increase their value proposition to their clients, and so forth.

Another approach is to look to your neighbors. Simply type your address in a search engine and do a search for nearby law firms, CPA firms, commercial lenders, HR consultants, and so forth. You can also look at your clients and their vendor relationships and then do a search within your local business community for these vendors as part of your pre-approach research.

After you have generated a list of firms, visit their websites to see whether their declared specialties match up with your expertise, your firm's expertise, and the major client densities within your book of business. For example, if you specialize in biotech, finding a law firm that has a biotech practice can be a very good thing and it facilitates mutual trades over time; they might even be doing workshops. Look at their website and see how they market themselves.

You'll often see that they'll hold workshops consistently on various topics, which you might be able to contribute to as an insurance professional by discussing how carriers are starting to align with new legislation or dealing with new issues at the macro level. Firms that offer webinars and workshops are often starved for content, so these can be a great find. Approach them and let them know what kind of valuable content you can provide that would benefit their constituency and make them look great to those constituents and ask for fifteen minutes to speak at their next workshop. This is a great way to bolt onto a channel that has already been established. They're the ones paying for the venue and managing the invitations, and you would be showing up to speak. In this way you are presented in an elevated position to the constituency that is listening to your content, allowing you to gain access on a very favorable basis for furthering discussions with them that can lead to new business for you. That's where the sales process really begins—that is, with the ability to approach someone on a favorable basis.

Once you have decided on some appropriate firms to target, the next step is to meet with them informally and discuss concept, benefits, and how you can contribute to their business. Some people bring a capability presentation. Some of them bring a team chart. Some of them bring a prestige client listing so the other party can gain a sense of what accounts they can be introduced to in terms of trade. One very common disconnect on this issue is that you don't necessarily have to do trades. For those readers who are beginning their career or are in the early stages of it, understand that you don't have to have an equal trade of referrals in order to pursue these types of relationships. What you need to be able to do is to serve their constituent clients and make them look better to their clients by solving their clients' insurance problems. So don't be discouraged from pursuing these arrangements if you can't offer an "equal trade" for clients on a quid pro quo basis. What you need is to be able to provide value to their clients, reinforce and augment their value proposition, and make them look great to their clients—and that you can do!

Structuring Center-of-Influence and Strategic-Alliance Relationships

There are many ways to handle these relationships. Some people do like to do direct trades of business. Some pay referral fees from the first trade forward. I would usually try to structure it to begin paying each other a referral fee after the fifth trade. That formula served me well in my career because people often would get excited about such deals but they wouldn't actually materialize. For that reason, I liked to have some kind of a milestone where five referrals needed to happen before either party gets paid a referral fee, which gives both an incentive to focus on facilitating introductions to exceed that mutually agreed upon milestone.

I'd also recommend signing a mutual nondisclosure agreement. This fundamentally protects both parties from any issue that might relate to privacy, covenants, keeping client information secure, and so forth. It's a good way to do business. I'd also encourage a covenant not to compete. We've seen this many times over the years where, for example, a property casualty firm doesn't have a benefits practice and a benefits firm doesn't have a property casualty practice, and they'll start to work with one another and do mutual trades. Unfortunately, what tends to happen is once either firm starts to realize how much business there is, they think it would make sense to hire someone and launch their own department to handle the business and reel back the business they referred to the external partner. Human nature being what it is regarding this matter, I always liked to include a buy-out clause that specifies if the amount of business justifies creating their own department and they wish to sever the relationship and take the business in-house, then they need to buy it back at a 1.5 multiple. That way everyone gets what they want. If they want that business back to develop their own internal practice, great! You get paid for it and can move on. This clause eliminates a lot of chaos, and, if they refuse to sign it, that is a great indication that there was another agenda present that is better to know up front than years later after you've done all the work.

To develop these relationships to their full potential, it's important to celebrate successes. Every time you generate a success for any referring entity, illuminate it. These types of arrangements speak the language of success. The referring party doesn't want to hear how troublesome the client they sent your way was. They want to hear something like this: "Well, they had some issues, and I can understand how their incumbent broker couldn't resolve them. We were able to resolve them successfully and they're very happy and thank you for the introduction to us." Perfect!

You also want to create monthly forums, workshops, and "lunch and learns" as collaborative venues to share ideas and make introductions. The idea is to create some type of structure or game plan where you are constantly engaging that entity throughout the year so they can gain more exposure to your work and the outcomes you can generate, which will then lead to more and more business over time. Also, developing a monthly or quarterly networking mixer and encouraging all of your center-of-influence and strategic-alliance partners to attend along with your clients and prospects is a great thing to do. Make sure it's at a place and time of day so people can congregate at your event easily and conveniently. Ultimately we're trying to put our fingerprint on the local business community by holding and sponsoring an event where people who are in new business development and hold portfolios of clients can meet each other, talk shop, and potentially do trades.

If you are ambitious enough to launch such an initiative, I can share with you from my own experience that these tend to pay off fabulously over time. However, they do tend to have a sales cycle of perhaps twelve to eighteen months to generate the first success. Don't get discouraged! Those who stick with it usually experience phenomenal success beginning in the two to two-and-a-half year range and have consistent payoff each year following for their efforts in building these relationships.

Selling through people via center-of-influence and strategic-alliance relationships is a key to serving the exponential growth of your practice. Many producers neglect this method of business development and suffer as a result. Developing these relationships allows you to further your reach. Pursue these relationships systematically, and in time you will be surprised by the impact.

Questions to Assess Center-of-influence and Strategic-Alliance Relationships

- What am I doing to develop more center-of-influence business?
- How am I supporting my agency in developing strategic-alliance-partner business?
- What am I doing to create monthly forums, workshops, and lunch and learns as collaborative venues to share ideas and make introductions between center-of-influence relationships and my client base?
- Have I developed a monthly (or quarterly) networking mixer?
- What am I doing in collaboration with center-of-influence and strategic-alliance partners to create a recurring event that impacts the culture within my local business community?
- Do I know who the vendors are for my top ten clients?
- Do I know what law firms, CPA firms, and commercial bankers in my local business community specialize in the same industries I am actively pursuing for new business opportunities?

CHAPTER 11

EIGHT THINGS NO ONE TALKS ABOUT THAT MAKE ALL THE DIFFERENCE IN THE SALE

I n this chapter we'll discuss some of the overlooked challenges to being awarded a piece of business. Some of these are big picture and some are little picture, but, ultimately, all are important. By keeping these issues in mind as you pursue business, you will experience greater success in turning prospects into satisfied clients.

1. The Value of Understanding the Workplace

Keeping in tune with the business environment is critical. Blogs and other online resources are great for understanding how the workplace is changing and what adaptations your buyers are making to both preserve and expand their own careers within their corporate hierarchies. Understanding and accounting for the inherent challenges your buyers face as they navigate their own careers within given entities and the overall workplace will contribute to your ability to win business.

Most people are hired and retained on the basis of their demonstrated self-reliance and proven track record of contributing results. Successful leaders are more empowering than powerful. They rely on their own competence (rather than just their authority) to get things done, and they expect you to do the same. Work security has shifted considerably and is now considered really a string of projects either within the same company or from company to company.

I was in the San Francisco Bay Area during my production career, and at that time the average HR director would be in their role about two years and seven months. The average CFO would be in their role three years and one month, and the average CEO for less than four years. This level of transiency means it's incumbent upon us to do a good job of keeping track of these individuals, supporting them in obtaining their next role when possible, and, at the very least, being notified when they achieve that next role. Connecting to the person who replaces them (letting them know that there was a game plan, you are generating results, and you'd like to keep their business for the sake of service continuity) is a critical skill to be mastered for the long-term success of any insurance professional. You must understand your own value and be able to communicate and demonstrate your work on demand as required. This is going to come up—and perhaps more often than you'd like it to—so master it.

2. Buyers Are Defensive

Buyer paranoia has become more and more pervasive, given the dynamics of our economy, and because of the aging of the boomers. It also is more prevalent as you move from Main Street to mid-market and eventually large market and "jumbo" business. Fundamentally, the bigger the account, the more you will see this operating in the buying decision.

Most mid-market and large market buyers are fairly defensive in their decision-making process and their buying preferences; quite frankly they don't want to make a mistake. They feel that if they choose the wrong broker, that it can be a reflection upon them. They are thinking of the vast human capital that exists within the marketplace wagging their tail and waiting for a new spot (i.e., *their* spot), and they don't want to be replaced.

Defensive buyers are concerned about risk as well as the cost of switching from one broker to another. To win their business, you need to address these issues. It's also important to remember that buyers represent groups of internal and external stakeholders whose needs and roles must be defined. Your primary buyer or advocate has people around them they need to please. You must account for that in your strategy in order to win their business.

Buyers will test the fences with a potential new vendor in more places with the assistance of technology than ever before—even before the formal courtship process begins! Remember that buyers work in high-stress environments and are pressed for time. If there are five brokers soliciting their business, one of the first things they'll do is look at LinkedIn® professional networking services and your company website and anything they can find through an Internet search. If you have a sparse LinkedIn® professional networking services profile and neither you nor your company have published anything in terms of white papers, case studies, and so forth, it's unlikely you'll make it through the vetting process. Understanding the defensive position of buyers is an often overlooked key to gaining business.

3. Professional Conduct

Genuine professional conduct speaks volumes. Be prepared! There is no excuse for lateness. Traffic jams and other issues beyond our control pop up from time to time, but preparation is the key to overcoming those issues. You don't want to start the meeting by apologizing for being late. It automatically puts you in a subordinate position and then you're playing defense. Some people I know schedule themselves to arrive fifteen to thirty minutes early and sit in their car and write notes and questions that they want to ask to collect themselves before the formally scheduled meeting time. Beautiful!

Research, which we have talked about extensively, remains a critical element for live and in-person meeting preparation. You need to arrive at the meeting prepared with well-informed questions. If you're asking someone to spend time in a face-to-face meeting, using a little bit of your time beforehand doing research is a good investment and helps to convey your respect for their valuable time.

If you are conducting a meeting with a prospect and your team members, try to meet your team at a staging area near your prospect's office and arrive as a group to the presentation venue. Sometimes you may call upon numerous experts as part of your team to attend the meeting and speak to certain topics, which is great. Teams buy from teams and that's part and parcel of working with larger accounts that are more lucrative for you. Remember that best practice is for everyone to arrive at the same time. I was trained fairly classically to have one's team stand behind their chairs and wait for everyone on the other side of the table to sit down before you and your team sit down. I think that's a polished way to do business and it shows respect for others, which I am really big on.

Remember to never disagree with a colleague in the field. Often the discussions can be complex, with many hidden nuances. Even if a colleague says something completely wrong, let it go during the face-to-face meeting and patch it up afterwards. Simply follow up with an email and make the correction as a point of clarification while you are summarizing the meeting discussion and next steps. People want to buy from a cohesive team, so don't lose the business to a team that is presenting a unified front. Don't be a team that is fragmented and disagreeing in the field with each other in front of a potential new customer.

For team presentations it can be helpful to have an agenda with topics, the presenters' names, and the duration for each topic in minutes. It is also helpful to have one moderator for the team to keep things on track. We're trying to avoid people speaking over each other in an uncoordinated and unstructured manner. Also, a small but important matter of housekeeping is to turn your cell phone off and ask your team to do the same. I have been in some meetings where the moderator indicated that unless you have a family member who is in distress or is sick and might need to take a phone call as an emergency, please turn your phones off. I thought that was a nice way to do that and have repeated it successfully over the years since then. Professional conduct isn't difficult, and the payoff is tremendous. Pay attention to this!

4. Have a Plan B

Always be prepared with a plan B for your meeting. You want to bring spare parts: extra cords, batteries, pens, papers, business cards, and so forth. More important, it's always worth it to bring a backup copy of your presentation on a jump drive in case the email of your presentation to them didn't go through because transmission was too large or some other snafu. A jump drive also saves the day if the laptop that is running the presentation dies. I've seen it happen: someone forgets to charge their laptop and doesn't bring their charger cable.

Carry an eyeglass repair kit, a sewing kit, and a shoeshine kit in your car, or even in your own carryall. Dirty shoes or a missing button make the wrong impression, and if an eyeglass lens pops out, that can sideline you. The minimal investment required to carry these items with you is well worth it. It can also make sense to keep an extra tie or shirt or blouse as the case may be, either in your office or your car. If you spill something on your clothes at lunch, it shouldn't get in the way of a good meeting with a prospect in the afternoon. Imagine working over the course of a year to get to a meeting point; who wants to be sidelined by stained clothing? Having a plan B in place for these minor emergencies demonstrates preparation, and it makes the whole experience more peaceful.

5. Setting Up the Presentation

Whenever possible, visit the venue ahead of time. If that's not possible, ask about equipment and availability of IT if something goes wrong. Also, have your own IT person's cell phone number handy, and alert that person that you may call during the presentation for assistance. Be sure to let them know the window of time that you'll be presenting.

Upon arriving, set up your presentation, your notes, and your pens. Set your carrying cases behind you or between the seats. Don't spread everything you have all over the table. Mind your space and organize yourself accordingly. Part of your setup can be this little trick: When you're meeting even a just a few new people, it can be easy to forget a name. To help yourself, align their business cards in the order of the way they're seated so you can remember who is who.

Seating arrangements are an important aspect of setup. Never sit right next to your prospect. Some people say if you sit on the same side of the table as your prospect, you're showing that you're on their side. I think that's hogwash. Best practice is to have your team on one side of the table and theirs on the other. Have your team sit either to your left or your right. Don't sit in the middle of your team. For eight or more at the table, I encourage you to take the foot of the table and leave the head of the table to buyers and the pecking order of their team to them. Basically, you want to be on the caboose so you can observe everything at the table—your team, their team, and the individual in charge.

If they leave the head of the table open, leave it open. Some firms don't even put a chair at the head or foot of the table. If they leave it open and there's a chair there, don't occupy it. Some producers like the feeling of being at the head of the table because they feel that implies they're in charge, but I've seen that backfire more times than I've seen it succeed so I discourage it.

If they offer you coffee or water, volunteer to go help them get it. And when the presentation is over, don't leave garbage, empty cups, or anything else on the table for them to pick up and throw away. Do it yourself even if it means washing your cup in their kitchen and putting it back in the cupboard. It just sends the right message: you are there to serve them, not the other way around.

6. Sequencing with Competitors

There are many different ways to look at sequencing, and there are certainly some differences in its application to writing Main Street business versus mid-market business. I'm going to focus on the mid-market segment here. In my view, it favors the business developer to be last to do the discovery meeting and first to perform the final presentation.

Let's assume there are three brokers vying for the business: the incumbent broker, another broker, and you. If you are the last to do discovery and you are successful in adding something or offering up an idea or shift in position regarding the buyer's preferences, it can be a great benefit to you. In other words, if they say, "We're telling all the brokers that we want an apple, an orange, and a pear," and you are the last to do discovery and say, "You know what? I understand that you want an apple, an orange, and a pear but I think you'll be a lot better off with an apple, a watermelon, and a pear," then you may have just shifted things. If you are successful in tweaking or readjusting their buying paradigm, it means the other brokers vying for that account are looking for an apple, an orange, and a pear when now the buyer wants an apple, a watermelon, and a pear. One of my favorite strategies as a broker was to always try to nudge the buying paradigm and be the last person to do that so that the others were pursuing the wrong tangent. By doing so, the others would deliver recommendations that were no longer in line with what the buyer wanted given their assignment of value to what I introduced to them as being in their best interest.

The benefit of being the first person to present is that it sets the standard. Find out when the last broker presents and when they are going to make a decision in order to "drip" the prospect with communications and exhibits of your work product during that process. Follow up and monitor how the others did. Try to compel a debrief: "You want to make a decision on January 20th and the last broker comes in on January 15th to make their presentation, so can we set up a debrief call on January 19th to go over any questions that you may have prior to you making your final decision?" Whenever possible, try to be the last person they speak with prior to making their decision.

I have found this to be a very effective strategy. You may find a different sequence that works for you, but understanding the implications of any given sequence is important in these matters. Give it some thought and find what best advances your practice. You may not always have a choice, but, if you do, it's good to be prepared and know what is most advantageous to you. If you ask 100 percent of your prospective clients for a specific sequence of events that you prefer in terms of discovery, presenting, office visitations, debriefs, and so forth, and only 30 percent of them grant it to you, then let's face it, that is a 30 percent advancement in gaining an advantage for your new business development situations over your competition. Ask!

7. Answering Questions about the Competition

When it comes to questions about the competition, it is best to take the high road. If you've never heard of them, just say you're unfamiliar with their work. Never slam a competitor. Never speak to their capabilities, strengths, weaknesses, or programs, and certainly don't get roped into a comparison between you and them. If you allow that to happen, you actually become a salesman for your competitor. Furthermore, you could easily provide incorrect information about your competitor, and then you've basically given the prospect misinformation, which will derail your progress. Avoid that at all cost. If someone asks for a comparison, it is better to simply answer why people do business with you. Speak to your strengths and suggest categories of comparison to the prospect that can make sense.

Educate your buyer on key categories of services, resources, capabilities, and so forth. You can point these matters out knowing that when the potential buyer asks the same questions of your competition that they will essentially hang themselves! That's a more effective way to address the competition. It's best to essentially say, "I'm not qualified to faithfully and accurately represent what the competition is doing but I am qualified to faithfully and accurately represent what we are doing so let's talk about that!" This is a much better approach and that's how you come out the winner when you are asked that question over the long haul.

8. Control the Environment after the Final Presentation to the Closing

From my perspective, the close is made after the final presentation. I think of the time period between our final presentation and when they will actually make their decision as "the dark period." This is when they are evaluating others and comparing and contrasting you and the other vendors who are competing for their business. Of course they are also weighing all the internal political considerations and other business factors before they make a decision and move forward with a given vendor. Drip messaging during this time is key. Send good news, send successes. You can even have clients call the decision maker during this time period and recommend you. You want to manage this period of time, not just sit around the office and wait. Keep your hands on the steering wheel. Invite them to your office, to an event, to a baseball game, or to a mixer. Manufacture any opportunity that you can to take a litmus test to gauge where they are in the decision-making process. Manage this phase aggressively.

Always reinforce positions or magnify positions taken during the process and never introduce something new. If you introduce something new during this phase, it's unlikely you will get the business. It's common to think about adding more new things to the conversation after your final presentation since the time is there, but in my view that's a mistake. Better to corroborate and reinforce the trajectory that you have consistently taken so far. When you make a deviation or a course correction, they may wonder what else they are missing. It will be viewed as if you're just throwing spaghetti on the wall to see if something sticks so you can get their business; that approach won't serve you or your potential client. You can provide testimonials, return on investment calculations, and case studies to provide more substance to the positions you've already taken, but nothing new unless you want to open up a big can of worms at the end and risk consternation, doubt, and all sorts of chaos, which most likely will lead to you not getting the business.

There is no better advice than the Boy Scout motto: "Be prepared." Do that and be on the lookout for items and issues that are easily overlooked and you will be ahead of the game. Ultimately, all of the issues we've discussed in this chapter impact sales. Some may seem nitpicky, but a sale is a sale. Don't let anything stand in your way.

Questions to Assess Often Overlooked Issues

- How effectively do I account for the interest and priorities of the different stakeholders for a given prospect?
- When I do joint work or cross-sell work with a colleague in the field, how well do I coordinate our presentation and messaging with them to a given prospect?
- How well am I prepared for a plan B in the field? Do I have spare parts?
- What is my standard answer about the competition?
- How do I manage the environment after the final presentation with the given prospect?

CHAPTER 12

THE TOP TEN MISTAKES PRODUCERS MAKE

E very year Rainmaker conducts a poll of our 12,000-plus subscribers, inquiring about their practice and how they grow it. We probe thirty different categories, and each year we publish the results, including the top ten most prevalent mistakes that our subscribers make, the damage those mistakes cause, and what can be done about them. The mistakes have a profound impact on the bottom line. Examine your practice as you read this chapter, and identify some areas to work on. I believe your time will be well spent in doing so.

Mistake #1: Lack of Cross-Sell between Disciplines

In our poll, 77 percent of the producers indicated that they received less than 5 percent of their new business from cross-selling activity, and 13 percent indicated that they received 5 to 20 percent of a contribution to their business from cross-selling activity. A best practice in terms of a cross-sell metric for an agency is somewhere between 18 and 22 percent—that's the contribution toward new business results each year from cross-selling activities. Clearly, 77 percent with less than 5 percent of new business from cross-selling indicates a major shortcoming.

This lack of cross-selling causes a lot of damage. First, there is the loss of new business revenues, and then there is the fact that retention suffers. The more lines of business with any given client, the higher the client retention rate. This issue not only impacts new business generation but also client retention.

One remedy for this can be organized by leadership doing some team building—getting producers around a table and identifying who does what and who does it well. One of the biggest disconnects that I've seen in my career is when the producers on one side of the house don't fully understand what the producers are doing on the other side of the house. To be specific, in many instances there are times when an agency has a very lucrative case on the property casualty side, but, when they would send it over to the employee benefit side of the house to write, there were only twenty employees or so and it was a fairly nominal case on that side of the house. It is also true that often a nominal case that is held by one side of the house isn't introduced to the other side of the house because they don't realize it can be a much more lucrative case to them than it is for themselves given the nature of the lines written. These kinds of issues are common. This is why getting producers around a table and having them identify the sweet spot for their business is so essential.

Another issue that crops up in cross-sell business is the reluctance a producer may feel to "give up the baby." If someone has courted that piece of business over a long period of time and it represents a significant percentage of their book of business, they want to make sure that the other side of the house will take care of it. Nobody wants to be embarrassed in front of one of their larger clients if the referral doesn't work out well. There is a risk inherent in this process. Again, a roundtable format will allow producers to talk about successes that they've generated for given clients in specific industries and circumstances. I personally was more comfortable sending a piece of business to the other side of the house toward somebody who had generated consistent successes in a given subject matter or a specific industry than toward someone who had not. The communication of cross-sell successes and favorable outcomes by the recipient will resonate with originating producers and make them feel more comfortable to send valuable business to the other side of the house. So the promotion of successes and the showcasing of work is important within production teams to enable more cross-sell business.

You can also administer this issue through a cross-sell matrix. Identify the top twenty-five accounts held by your organization and reference across all lines of coverage sold by your organization. Really this is just a spreadsheet that lists who the client is, who derived it, where it originated, the lines of coverage they sold, and then the other lines of coverage that your agency has to offer that have yet to be placed with a given client.

Leadership should defer to the judgment of the originating producer about the timing of an introduction. Anyone who's managed a client over a number of years knows that sometimes you're the hero and sometimes you're the villain, depending on rate increases or a claim issue that has been dragging on too long, and so forth. This is why the originating producer should drive the timing of an introduction.

Ultimately, aside from roundtable discussions and using a formal cross-sell matrix, developing relationships with the other side of the house and generating wins for them is key. Successes should be celebrated, which will increase confidence and hopefully generate more cross-sell activity.

Mistake #2: Lack of Sales Pipeline Management

In our poll we asked, "Do you manage a sales pipeline to track active prospects?" and 16 percent of respondents indicated "never," while 34 percent of respondents indicated "sometimes."

The problem here is the inability to predict future revenues. If you think about a producer as a microeconomic unit within the macro entity (the agency or the brokerage), they should be able to provide a reasonable estimate of new business coming in within the next ninety days. Consider that if you were a publicly traded company and your stockholders asked, "What do you think your projected revenue will be next quarter?" it would be unacceptable to answer that you have no idea. If you did, investors would most likely sell their stock in your company. So the ability to predict future revenues vis-à-vis a pipeline tool is a critical element for any producer navigating their career within the insurance industry.

Another issue is that without managing a pipeline, you're unable to make adjustments to improve the sales process. When you work a pipeline, there are many stages to manage and measure. This is what allows you to discover if there is a blockage going from one stage to the next, which would require a remedy. Absent of measuring a pipeline and understanding movement through the different stages, it becomes challenging to make improvements and adjustments to your sales process that will help you win more new business.

Another issue with a lack of pipeline management is it hinders the ability to establish a critical path and communicate processes to potential customers. As producers move from Main Street business to mid-market business, the ability to articulate a process becomes more and more important. Purchasing officers from mid-market businesses want to know the steps in the process, how long it takes, and how those steps serve their desired outcomes.

This also comes into play in your attempts to derive prospective clients from a center-of-influence relationship. Imagine, for example, a center of influence who owns a law firm, saying, "I'd like to refer business to you. Can you just tell me the process that the people I refer to you will go through?" Only a clear and specific articulation of the process will give that center of influence the confidence to send business your way. So a lack of a methodology not only impacts your ability to convince prospects to change their insurance program, but it also impacts your ability to get referral business from center-of-influence relationships that you've developed over time.

The remedy, certainly, is to establish an easy-to-use pipeline that identifies the following: contact information, estimate of commission per account, and the source of the business. Was it through an introduction? Was it through LinkedIn® professional networking services? Was it through attending a specific business mixer? Where did it come from? The pipeline should outline the stages of your sales process and where each prospect is within those stages. It should include a look at weighted closing percentage based on stage. This is fundamentally assuming somebody at the beginning of the sales process has maybe a 10 or 20 percent chance of closing, and someone who has gone through a lengthy process with you, just by sheer fact that they hung in there, has a higher percentage of closing, maybe 60 or 70 percent.

The pipeline should also tie next steps to each prospect. Early in my career one of my coaches talked about the difference between a good idea and a great idea, and he would always tell me, "David, a great idea is simply a good idea with an action plan attached to it!" Good ideas are one thing, but if there is no next step, it's simply going to sit there in a stage of the sales process and not move on. Total commissions, total gross opportunity volume, and net commissions all contribute to your ability to discern an estimate of future commissions that most likely will be forthcoming from your current efforts.

I know that the concept of managing a sales pipeline isn't very popular among many producers because the moment that they complete a record inside their company's CRM, they feel like leadership will never stop asking them when the deal will close. My advice is that it's okay to run concurrent pipelines. You can certainly manage the one that your company uses, but we have seen that more than 70 percent of the multimillion-dollar producers in the industry manage their own separate pipeline, one that speaks to them, serves them, and keeps them on track. So there are two—one for the company and one for them—running concurrently at all times.

Mistake #3: Failure to Update Sales Pipeline Weekly
In our poll we asked, "How often do you update your new business pipeline to reflect changes in the sales process of a given prospect or to add new prospects into the pipeline?" and 50 percent indicated at least once a month; only 36 percent indicated they did so at least once a week.

This failure to update the pipeline causes real damage: nearly two-thirds of total opportunities are forgotten without weekly record keeping. This is especially true for veterans, and any producers with a large book of business. You have so much flying at you throughout the week in terms of issues as it relates to managing your book of business that it's easy to forget about somebody you met at a function or someone who may have been introduced to you by a client or center of influence.

In our experience working with producers through our coaching programs, we have learned that nearly two-thirds of the total opportunities that came across their desk in any given week were forgotten. Furthermore, nearly half of the prospects that they did record had no next step or action item established to move them from one stage to the next within their pipeline and sales process.

Do the math. Without weekly recordkeeping, we forget two-thirds of the opportunities and, for those that we actually do remember, only half have an action item or a next step, which means, fundamentally, that most producers operate at perhaps one-sixth of their total potential. That is an extreme number, but I will say this: I've seen many reports in the industry where large organizations that implemented a pipeline for the first time experienced increased sales north of 38 percent. The act of consistently updating a pipeline *will* increase your sales; it's a proven fact. It's not fun to do, but it works and will contribute to the growth of your practice.

Best practice is to update a pipeline weekly. We encourage our clients to make that their last act on a Friday, because that way they're able to capture all of the things that occurred during the week while they are still fresh in their mind. Update your pipeline every Friday, print it out, and then go home and relax, without worrying over the weekend that you may have missed an opportunity that can lead to the growth of your book. Our clients who do this religiously report that they are capturing more opportunities, moving more business through their pipeline, and are able to clear their head and relax over the weekend.

The remedy, again, is to establish one day per week to update the pipeline and tie next steps appropriate to each prospect for tasking the following week. I believe best practice is to do this on a Friday afternoon or even Saturday mornings, so you can capture everything that happened that week and relax! Going in and out of your company's CRM after every phone call or meeting can be a bit challenging; I advise printing it out each week and scribbling notes on it to keep it updated. Then go into the CRM once a week, update your pipeline with the notes, and print out a fresh copy. That's best practice and saves time.

Mistake #4: Not Developing and Managing Focused Sales Campaigns

In our poll we asked, "Do you develop and manage sales campaigns targeted to key industries or specific prospect demographics and criteria?" and 53 percent of the respondents indicated yes, while 47 percent indicated no.

Let's evaluate the damage from this. Most of us, when we start our career, will write any relationship that we have, whether they are a VP of HR for a high-tech company or the owner of a yogurt shop. We tend to write a very eclectic and broad range of industries because we're really scaling our business through our existing relationships regardless of what industry they are in; we call this "anything and everything" or A&E marketing. But there comes a point in our careers when A&E marketing only gets us so far, specifically a book of business that is generating about a $300,000–400,000 of annual commissions, and that tends to be the peak for most with this marketing methodology. To move beyond that, producers need to develop verticals, specialties, and sales campaigns. Without these, producers can't establish themselves as experts in a given transaction type, and that's what really helps generate the larger books of business in our industry.

One of my early mentors told me, "Any road leads to nowhere." That means if you are a generalist and just going wherever your relationships take you, you're not going to be as successful over time as somebody who declares a specialty in a few areas and actively drives those verticals.

The remedy is to establish and promote the one thing that you're great at. It could be an industry niche. It could be a situation like divestitures. Or it could be a pervasive problem, such as a work site safety program that isn't functioning correctly. Part of establishing a niche is understanding your firm's ideal business. Basically you want to understand at the macro level what your firm can do and then, within that, at the micro level what niches you can specialize in within the mothership's appetite for business that will differentiate you and help you win more business over time.

Mistake #5: Lack of a Drip Campaign

In our polled we asked, "Have you established a drip campaign and use it for both new business development as well as to increase client retention?" and 32 percent of respondents indicated yes, while 68 percent of respondents indicated no.

Let's assess the damage. Statistically, we know that only 12 percent of buyers will engage us on the first attempt. In other words, 88 percent are simply not ready to buy yet. What are they doing? They are establishing us as a future resource in case a material agent of change occurs within their business that gives rise to the suspicion that they will outgrow their current broker. An example would be a small firm that is working successfully with a small agency, but they perhaps are looking around for financing, which will allow them to establish new locations across the United States; in that case, their "single location broker" might not be able to attend to them at that size with so many locations. They are vetting brokers ahead of time in case the material event manifests. This is a period to manage skillfully with a drip campaign. Send the prospect case studies, white papers, quotes, testimonials, and work exhibits over time so that you become bigger and more credible in their eyes than when you first came into contact. Then, when they're actually ready to buy, you have escalated your value proposition from the original exchange and you are more appealing to do business with than ever before.

Without a drip campaign, you're probably not taking advantage of the accumulated inventory of people you've met and the organizations that will buy when they are ready. We see this a lot with veterans who have amassed huge contact lists over the years but they're not keeping in touch with them. There's a lot of out of sight, out of mind at work here with prospective clients; we have to do something to stay on their radar.

The remedy is to establish at least four to six communications per year. There's a lot of data out there on this subject, and it suggests that if we touch somebody fewer than four times per year, we might as well not reach out to them at all. A bit surprising, right? We believe the sweet spot is somewhere between quarterly and once per month. So essentially four to twelve "touches" per year. We do recognize some entities provide a monthly newsletter, which is fine, but the only way to measure whether we're reaching out too often is by looking at how many people unsubscribe from these newsletters or other direct communications we issue throughout a given year.

Empirically we know that reaching out fewer than four times per year is ineffective. At the qualitative level, I would advise that you sell the way you want to be sold to. If you like receiving updates and communications every other month, do that. If you like to receive those once a month, do that. Do weekly communications from others bother you?

If so, then don't do that! Use your gut instinct to determine the right frequency of messaging and use the modalities that would resonate with you: email, faxes, calls, stopping by their office, and so forth.

Mistake # 6: Not Using Technology to Stay Informed about Agents of Change

In our poll we asked, "Do you use technology to help you identify agents of change within a business or with changes in a purchasing officer's status that can assist with making a sale?" and 3 percent indicated yes, while 97 percent indicated no. Clearly there's a lot of room for improvement here.

The use of any free online technology service that will automate an Internet search for you and keep you apprised of new developments is vital to the new business developer. With these services, you can name an individual or company or whatever, and it will notify you of a change in its status—whether that's a press release, a comment, a review, a lawsuit, or anything else. It's a valuable tool, and, again, most of them are free and easy to set up.

Without using these tools, you lose the ability to act on a timely basis as agents of change arise within a prospective client's situation during the course of the year. You also cannot track when a competitor shifts position or changes its service platform. This is something we see a lot, and it's important to track, because it reveals opportunities that are ripe for picking.

Similarly, someone who insisted on using a particular broker at a firm you had been courting may leave their position and go to another firm. This event can open the door for you to work with someone else at that firm who wanted to do business with you but was prevented from doing so by the individual who just departed. Set up auto-notifications to receive sector reports on different industries and to track specific companies to see if they have raised capital or are expanding. You could also monitor their perceived threats to growing their business and align your initial messaging and outreach marketing programs in line with some of those major concerns. All of this will allow you to send appropriate messaging, which will hopefully culminate in a sale.

Mistake #7: No Dedicated Time for Prospecting

In our poll we asked, "Do you set aside specific time each week for prospecting?" and 61 percent indicated yes, while 39 percent indicated no.

The damage done here is that by neglecting new business development, you potentially experience deep production troughs between sales cycles and fail to reach production goals and achieve your full potential throughout the year.

To remedy this, we recommend establishing four days per week with two-hour block minimums for prospecting. The fifth day is a spill day that is either used to catch up on a prospecting session that was missed or as a respite from prospecting. In other words, we encourage as a best practice for all our clients to use two-hour blocks Monday through Thursday and vary the timing. In other words, don't do it every morning, because there's a group of buyers out there that are so busy in the morning that they only have time to engage someone in a discussion in the afternoon, and vice versa.

A best practice would look something like this: Monday afternoon, Tuesday morning, Wednesday afternoon, Thursday morning. Friday is basically a spill day, dedicated to administrative work, talking to underwriters, talking to your team, talking to leadership, getting ready for the next week, updating your pipeline, and so forth. Or, if something hijacked one of your prospecting time slots during the week, then you could use two hours on Friday to make up the time. Don't be afraid to dedicate the time on your calendar and schedule around it. You'll be surprised by how flexible other demands upon your time are when you actually block out this time on your calendar.

Mistake #8: Insufficient Hours Dedicated to New Business Development

In our poll we asked, "In a typical week, how many hours do you spend focused on new client generation? This can include direct calling, asking for introductions, attending business mixers, lunches with centers of influence, social events, and so forth." Nineteen percent of respondents indicated they spend two hours or less per week in new client generation, 26 percent indicated three to five hours a week, 26 percent indicated six to ten hours, and 19 percent indicated eleven to twenty hours. Only 10 percent of producers spent more than twenty hours on new business development, and those were primarily developmental producers with no real books to manage, giving them the ability to spend so many hours of their week prospecting. The damage caused by not dedicating enough hours per week for new business development is plain, simple, and extensive: failure to achieve objectives.

The remedy is to not only dedicate time on the calendar for prospecting efforts but to create sustainability by mixing up new business development activity in order to keep things fresh. What you don't want to do is grind out the cold calling every day of the week. Vary it by day— direct calling, cold calling, attending a networking event or mixer, cold canvassing, center-of-influence development, webinars, and so forth. You can even have a day of asking for introductions from your network or through reviewing their connections on LinkedIn® professional networking services, thus providing them with a prompt vis-à-vis the names of individuals they are connected to that might be great customers for you. Keep things fresh and mix it up so you don't burn out.

Mistake #9: Lack of Center-of-Influence Development

In our poll we asked, "What percentage of your new business comes from center-of -influence relationships, which are external to your firm and that you've developed yourself?" and 34 percent of respondents indicated that less than 5 percent of their new business comes from center-of-influence development, while 31 percent indicated that between 5 and 20 percent of their new business comes from center-of-influence relationships and development. Only 9 percent indicated 21 to 30 percent, and roughly 25 percent indicated that more than half of their business comes through center-of-influence relationships. Most of those who said they received more than 50 percent of their new business from that modality are multimillion-dollar-book producers. As you can see, a hallmark of becoming a multimillion-dollar-book producer is center-of-influence development.

Without center-of-influence development, you fail to leverage relationships that surround the buyer and fail to ride channels that have already been established to the buyer by other service providers. The remedy is to identify your buyers and establish different paths to them. Who are all the vendors of an HR professional? Who are all the vendors of a CFO? Who are all the vendors of a COO? Who are all the vendors of a VP of corporate development? Whoever your primary purchasing agent is—whatever role they occupy within the firm—find their vendors and reach out to them. This is about finding who is connected to your ultimate buyer, someone you can develop a relationship with, establish credibility with, and perhaps do some trades with, who will then give you a favorable introduction to your target.

There are a number of ways to do this. You can certainly ask your top ten clients who their vendors are. The rest is pretty easy. Introduce yourself to them, and invite them to lunch or even for a formal meeting. You can both do capability presentations sharing with each other what your respective firms are doing, what kind of business you're looking for, where you've had successes, and then see if you can do trades. It's usually a pretty straightforward and easy process.

Mistake #10: Too Many Small Accounts

In our annual poll we asked, "What percentage of your book of business is composed of clients paying less than $5,000 in annualized commissions?" and 41 percent indicated that more than half of their book's revenue was made up of this kind of business, while 22 percent indicated that this type of business made up 5 to 20 percent of their book. There is a lot to be done here, and a lot should be done, because this can be very damaging to any producer's career over time. It is a natural act to dispense with the bottom part of your book of business, however you define it, periodically throughout your career.

The remedy is to look at the bottom segment of your book of business and ask yourself some questions. Are they growing? Are they a good ambassador for your firm? Are they making introductions to your target clients? Are they attached to the other side of the house where it is a significant piece of business? You should perform this test annually.

Keep those in your book that meet that test, and then either transfer the remainder out into an internal SBU or empower one of your account managers to run with it. Another option is to sell off that business to one of the entities out there in the industry that actually buys small books of business. That way you can re-capitalize your practice and use the money for more account management staff, raises, bonuses, or telemarketers. Regardless of how you handle it, scrub out the small accounts periodically throughout your career. Doing so always catapults a book forward—always.

In examining the biggest mistakes that producers make each year, we at Rainmaker hope to help producers see areas that they can address and develop that will help them move their practices forward. The ten mistakes we've examined in this chapter profoundly impact business development, and, therefore, sales revenue. Choose one of these mistakes to focus on, apply the remedy, and watch for an impact to your bottom line.

Questions for Assessing Your Mistakes

- Do I have a dedicated time and day each week to update my new business pipeline?
- Do I have auto-notifications set up to monitor my top ten clients and key prospects?
- How many of my clients' company pages do I follow on LinkedIn® professional networking services?
- What method(s) am I using to keep in touch with prospects between the first conversation and when they are ready to engage me?
- What am I doing to earn introductions and referrals with center-of-influence relationships in my community?
- Has the minimum size client I am willing to pursue remained the same over the past three years or has it increased?

SECTION 3: LEADERSHIP CONSIDERATIONS

CHAPTER 13

MAKING SALES MEETINGS COUNT

I f you own an agency, are currently in a sales leadership position, or you are a producer looking to migrate into a leadership role within your firm, conducting sales meetings is a critical skill to master. In this chapter we'll look at actionable items you can use to make your sales meetings more productive and successful.

Essentials for Successful Sales Meetings

Producers often feel like these meetings are a waste of time because they serve management and not producers. Some even say it feels like a trip to the woodshed. I was with one firm early in my career as a producer where we used to call it our monthly beating. Understanding these attitudes is an important foundation for conducting a good sales meeting.

Of course it is also helpful for anyone assuming the responsibility of conducting these meetings to step back and identify the desired outcome. What strategic objectives do you want the meeting to serve? It could be a celebration of achievement, or confirming the significance of a role to an organization, or keeping your producers sharp. The sharper you keep your producers—the more abreast of information, legislation, and competitor issues occurring in the marketplace—the better chance they will have to prevail over competition in the field.

Your tactical objectives should make up most of the agenda. Variable topics can be inserted or withdrawn over the course of the year based on what the enterprise-level objectives are. In other words, it might be a variable that in the first quarter the firm needs more cross-sell activity, in which case you would insert that topic as a variable. In the third quarter the firm might want stewardship calendars deployed for each of its top ten clients, in which case you would insert that topic as a variable. Sales meeting agendas should have standing categories of discussion that occur in every meeting that serve the overall strategic objective, as well as additional items that cater to the changes and issues that crop up throughout the year.

Here is an example of one possible standard agenda:

- Review of progress for action items issued in the previous meeting
- Most recent new business wins
- Top three new business opportunities
- Industry intelligence
- Competitor intelligence
- New sales initiatives being launched
- Agreed upon action items for the next meeting

In terms of variable items, during the course of the year, the following items might need to be addressed:

- Account-rounding opportunities
- Cross-sell opportunities
- Center-of-influence opportunities
- Most recent introductions
- Most recent testimonials and endorsements
- Service achievements
- Carrier or product updates
- Legislative updates
- Blogs or articles created and published

I have participated in hundreds of sales meetings throughout my career, both as a producer and as a practice leader, an office leader, and then a regional CEO for a large public brokerage. Ideally these meetings are a genuine discussion that stimulate critical thinking and generate ideas. Sales meetings should be about forty-five minutes. I recommend going around the table several times to have each person chime in for the various discussion points to keep it vibrant and engaging. I always liked to include one roundtable question for discussion at each meeting so producers could learn from one another.

Good roundtable discussion questions include the following:

- What verticals are paying the most dividends? Which ones are working, which ones aren't?
- What are you doing to differentiate yourself in the field?
- What methods are you finding to be the most effective in winning new business?
- How are you promoting your work in the field?
- What are your biggest challenges to writing more new business?
- What service successes are you promoting to generate introductions from those clients? What are your top three competitors doing to win more new business?
- What new verticals or new industries are reported to be the fastest growing?
- What are the most recent developments within your largest five clients?

Why Sales Meetings Matter

Here is some recent data from the annual poll that we conducted here at Rainmaker Advisory:

- 91 percent of producers have no clear target client definition
- 68 percent have no drip campaign
- 57 percent have no focused sales campaigns or key industry verticals
- 67 percent have gaps in prospecting methodologies
- 71 percent are not fully aware of their firm's resources
- 77 percent derive less than 5 percent of their business through cross-selling
- 64 percent do not update their pipeline every week
- 78 percent fail to leverage their large accounts

Sales meetings are the perfect opportunity to address these short-comings. As a sales leader, if you were to align your weekly or biweekly sales meeting agenda to address one or more of these topics throughout the course of a given year, chances are good you will strike a chord that resonates with others in the meeting. It's a great opportunity to help producers create a capability or increase their skills in a different area, which will then allow them to prevail in competitive environments and secure more new business.

As a consultant since 2008, I've spoken with so many agency owners who walk me through all of the resources and capabilities that their firm has, but when I ask producers if they're aware of those capabilities, a significant number are not. Use sales meetings to broadcast capabilities and resources. You can also ask those who have used those resources to discuss the results and successes they've had with them.

One of the benefits of a consistent agenda is that it helps everyone to come prepared. You don't want to carry the whole weight of the sales meeting on your back. You want the participants in that meeting to come to the table prepared to discuss the growth of their practice and how they will achieve the enterprise's objectives for the year.

If somebody has had a significant win, ask them, "How did you do it? Where did the business come from? How did you secure the first meeting? What were the challenges along the way? Who competed against you for the business? Where did the incumbent broker fall short? What were the solutions you presented?" This is great for those developing their career to hear as well as your veterans. Everyone can benefit from hearing about another producer's winning path.

Roundtable discussions are another valuable option that could be included on your agenda. Ask about common challenges associated with growing a book of business. This is a great way to get the knowledge your veterans hold out to your apprentice and mid-level producers. Also, I always like to encourage leaders to bring something to the table for the meeting. Keep the troops informed. It could be a white paper or an article or a case study. If you're reading something that would be useful to your team, copy it, distribute it, and talk about it at the meeting.

Meeting Logistics

Set up your sales meetings for the entire year. You could simply send an invitation to everyone for a meeting that will take place every other week for the upcoming year as a recurring meeting and use the meeting description to place your standing agenda so everyone knows what will be discussed every time and can come prepared. That way it's on everyone's calendar. You could also consider varying the frequency by season, since the calendar year can vary in intensity. Some people feel it's most effective to do these sales meetings every other week throughout the year. I think a very good case could be made for holding meetings once a week during the first three months of the year, every other week throughout the next six months, and once a month during the last three months. It's healthy to provide a cadence or a rhythm. It's okay to take pauses around holidays. It's okay to pause in the month of August when your producers might be less available due to family vacations. Every sport has a pre-season, season, post-season and of course an off-season. It's wise to consider this and vary the frequency of your meetings in accordance with the seasons of your agency's year.

I encourage you to consider distributing the meeting agenda three days prior to the event and ask if anyone wants to add anything. This sends the message that you want to serve your producers and help them grow their book. Soliciting feedback and asking about anything that they specifically want to talk about for an upcoming meeting is good leadership.

Some leaders like to review pipelines prior to these meetings. I think this is great as long as you don't have the intention of making this a witch hunt and using the information you gathered to beat someone up at the meeting! I do think it's important for a leader to do a last-minute sweep of people's pipelines. Then if you do hear something in the meeting being offered up by a producer, you can kind of get a sense of what's going on based on their pipelines and have some background about it so you can ask better questions or better offer support to them in securing the opportunity they are referencing in the meeting.

As a leader, you should arrive fifteen minutes early to the meeting. Here's why: I have seen cultures where the producers congregate and chitchat and wait for the leader, who comes late to the meeting. The real message when a leader is late to a sales meeting is that it's not that important and the leader doesn't really want to be there. By showing up fifteen minutes early, you are demonstrating that the meeting is a priority. Then, I would encourage you to stay fifteen minutes afterwards. I've seen many leaders be the first to leave when they conduct these meetings, which again sends the message to the troops that this person doesn't really want to be there. Arrive early, leave late.

Distribute agendas on the conference table while you're waiting for everyone to arrive. Don't take time during the meeting to distribute papers. Instead, set the meeting up for your producers, and start the meeting exactly on time. I know some leaders wait for their top producers to arrive, and they might arrive five or ten minutes late. The problem with starting the meeting late to accommodate late arrivals is that you're penalizing the people who were responsible and respectful enough to show up on time. Start right on time. Review the agenda and ask for any questions. It's okay to say, "Here's what we're going to talk about. Does anyone else want to add to the agenda? Speak now or forever hold your peace." Proceed through the agenda. I always liked to take my watch off, put it right next to me, and watch the time so we could get through the entire agenda and conclude the meeting on time as promised.

Be sure to save time on your schedule to solicit feedback and thoughts after the meeting. I always liked to ask, "What was your take-away? What are you going to put into practice? What are you going to start with? We talked about ten things. Give me three things that really resonated with you and give me one thing you're going to give a whirl for next week. What are you going to try?" Also always entertain new ideas for the next meeting.

Part of your role as a leader in these meetings is to make sure that the team maintains the cadence and addresses the issues that enable the growth of their practice. It's also important to maintain awareness of everyone's time and the need to bring the meeting to a timely conclusion. As the meeting proceeds, it's okay to let everyone know there are just thirty minutes remaining, fifteen minutes remaining, and then, lastly, five minutes remaining. That gives everyone a sense that you're being respectful of their time and you are doing your best as the moderator to move along things along and conclude on time. If you run out of time for an agenda item or two, just say, "You know what, we didn't have time to cover these two items, but we will cover them first thing at the next meeting. Have a great day, everyone."

Meeting Conduct

Meeting conduct is a topic that's frequently overlooked. First and foremost: Don't beat up on anyone or humiliate anyone. Champion a respectful environment. Be gracious and kind, and give praise and recognition at every opportunity to do so. Really what you want to create is a nurturing environment. That might sound a little strange, but give some thought to producer psychology. If someone has a 30 percent closing ratio, 70 percent of their world is failure. If someone has a 40 percent closing ratio, 60 percent of their world is failure. The most beneficial tactic is to make sure these meetings are nurturing, healing, and affirming. Be positive. If there is a specific instance in which you need to offer constructive criticism or help somebody who's off track get back on track, that conversation is much better suited to a one-on-one meeting rather than the sales meeting. Remember the old adage: Praise in public, punish in private.

Sometimes problems arise during meetings. If somebody says something that's a little wonky or bizarre, don't criticize them personally. It's okay to challenge the assertion or point of view that they are offering up, but don't criticize them personally. Keep it professional. If people are being disruptive or unprofessional, put an end to it because you need to protect the learning environment for others at the table. Be forthright. Simply say, "We do these meetings to advance your book of business and help you all make more money. Disruptive and nonproductive comments are counter to our culture and a waste of everyone's time, and I want you to stop." Just lay it out there for them and leave no doubt.

A really helpful tool is the phrase, "Let's discuss that offline." You can use it to get out of uncomfortable pickles that can be part of this process. If somebody offers up something that is incongruent with the spirit of the meeting you're holding, you can say, "You know what, that's a great comment. How about you and I take that offline?" Continue with your agenda without being derailed by something that might not be productive to discuss in an open forum.

When dealing with people's ideas, it's good to be up front about what will be pursued in the near future. You can say, "You know what, those were great ideas, and I agree with all of them, but right now here are our key priorities for the next six months. Once we accomplish those priorities, then we will revisit the ideas you are offering up and decide how to act."

After the Meeting

Of course, you want to thank everyone for attending, but, from my experience, if you have multimillion-dollar-book producers on your team or if you have some superstars on your team, it's okay to reach out to them personally afterwards and say, "Hey, thanks for showing up to that meeting." When I ran Northern California for USI Holdings, I had six offices scattered across Northern California and sometimes producers would drive an hour or two, or even three hours, to attend a sales meeting depending upon the subject matter. The sheer fact that a multimillion-dollar-book producer is showing up to a sales meeting speaks volumes to your mid-level producers and certainly your developmental producers, and that should be recognized. Simply tell them, "Hey, I really appreciate you showing leadership by attending this meeting. Frankly, when others see you doing that, then they realize there's no excuse for them not doing it themselves, so thank you." A little bit of that goes a long way in terms of culture.

Inform producers who missed the meeting that they can get information regarding what was discussed from their colleagues. Time is precious, and the most efficient use of your time is simply to direct anyone who missed out to ask one of their peers that did attend the meeting. There's no reason for you to have one-on-ones with every producer that misses a sales meeting. Lastly, send a summary email, restating what was discussed, what action items came out of the meeting, and giving praise and recognition to various individuals who attended and reported achievements in a couple of bullet points.

Cultural Fit

Finding the right formula for your sales meeting has to reconcile a lot of things: strategic objectives of the firm, tactical objectives, how to execute, culture, and tenure classifications. Chances are you will have a mix of producers—from those in the developmental stage to those in their twenty-fifth year and beyond. Be sure to account for that as you plan and conduct your meetings.

You also need to account for performance classes. We've worked with agencies here at Rainmaker that have two hundred producers or more and their top thirty producers have multimillion-dollar books. Those producers are looking for something different from a meeting than the middle or the bottom layer. It's okay to create different sales meetings for producers with different performance classifications of new business run rates or size books. In other words, it's okay to conduct different sales meetings that speak to different segments of producers within your firm if, practically speaking, there are enough producers in each category to hold a separate meeting for.

It's important for you to consider the number of participants in a meeting. There's a lot of different data out there about the subject. I think the magic number is somewhere between the range of eight and fifteen. As you go above that it starts to squelch people's comfort level in offering things up. I don't think a sales meeting with a hundred people in it is very productive for anyone. We want to solicit feedback and learn what they need from us as leaders to help them grow their practice. I have seen that work in meetings with up to thirty-five, but give some thought to the number that is in line with your culture. If your meeting starts to get too big and is squelching participation given its size, then you need to start splitting up meetings by tenure classification, book size, new business run rate, practice specialty, or whatever works for your organization.

If sales meetings are new to your culture but you'd like to begin holding them, start slowly. It's a mistake to superimpose a very mature sales management structure right out of the gate when nothing has existed previously. If your firm has not traditionally had sales management or sales meetings, begin with incremental steps. If you don't, you'll induce culture shock, and some producers may even resign, which naturally creates a lot of chaos and is something to avoid. When you're implementing such a program from scratch, the idea is progress, not perfection. Where is everyone now? What is the next immediate step forward? There might be ten, twelve, or twenty steps after that that lead to developing and implementing a fully robust and mature sales management structure, but give your people time to adjust. Once they do, then add another element and then another. Over time it will come together to everyone's benefit.

Remember sales meetings are about your team, not about you. I've seen some leaders spend the first fifteen minutes of these meetings talking about their vacation or golf game. Producers have tremendous demands upon their time. They're stretched in all sorts of ways. I always like to start meetings saying, "I know your time is precious. We're going to talk about these things today and I'll do the best I can to earn your time today."

I really mean that: Earn your team's time, attention, and attendance by holding a high-quality meeting. Always have standing items, variable items, and a roundtable discussion question so that everyone can come to the meeting prepared. As a leader, your people will look where you look. Use the meetings to illuminate the issues that serve your agency's business drivers. And don't forget: Praise in public, punish in private.

Questions to Assess Sales Meeting Activity

- What do I want the team's takeaways to be and the assignment of value toward these meetings to be?
- After the meetings do they have a better idea of our resources and capabilities?
- Have they heard a success story?

- Have they had an opportunity to express some challenges about a common issue that occurs in new business development and discuss that with their peers so they can sit down at their desk with a new skill?
- What value have I provided?
- Have I earned their time?

CHAPTER 14

SALES LEADERSHIP—WHAT IT'S ALL ABOUT

There is a general sentiment in the insurance industry that producers cannot make good leaders, and I believe that premise is categorically false. In this chapter we will discuss sales leadership to both help those already in a sales leadership role as well as for producers who are interested in making the leap to leadership. If you are a producer who wants to move into a leadership role, this chapter will guide you into the responsibilities for advancing the wealth and prosperity of the producers within your constituency. If you are already a sales leader, this chapter should help you refine areas where you can apply your efforts that will be in the best interest of your team's overall prosperity.

Let's begin by looking at some helpful questions:

- How are you helping your colleagues become dedicated students of the insurance industry?
- How are you helping your colleagues experience progressively greater achievements year over year?
- How are you helping your colleagues find their authentic sales path?
- How are you helping your colleagues manage themselves as microeconomic business units, and what are you doing to empower them within their roles?
- How are you providing a framework and a cadence to help your colleagues stay on track as they progress towards their goals?

In my experience, if you align your efforts toward addressing these key questions, that should get you and your team over the finish line more often than not.

Helping Your Colleagues Become Students of the Industry

A good start here would be to work with your colleagues to understand the different segments within the retail insurance broking distribution channels—sole proprietorships, agencies, regionals, nationals, boutique and consulting firms, and the globals. Within each segment there tends to be a sweet spot—which we refer to as a footprint. The footprint reflects three fundamental aspects: the ability to acquire a new piece of business, the ability to keep that business over time, and the market's perception of a given platform's ability to be a faithful custodian and effective steward of their business over time.

When we look at segmentation, we see that a sole proprietor can acquire a very small case profitably due to low overhead. It could be $500 of net commissions and fees (NCF) for a given case, and they will typically tend to write as their largest account possibly $40,000–50,000 of NCF. An agency might have a minimum of $2,500 or even $5,000 of NCF because of greater operational expenses, and because there are more resources within the team, their platform might reach to cases that generate over $100,000 of NCF. The numbers go progressively higher for the other segments. Every different segment has its own ability in terms of its effectiveness in acquiring cases in specific NCF ranges. What we must understand as new business developers is that each segment is aligned toward a given customer or target market space. And, in some ways, different sales methodologies are applicable to different segments given differences in buying preferences and the existence of varying resources available to meet those preferences within each segment.

Of course, there are hundreds of sales methodologies and philosophies out there, but I think a reasonable case can be made for three different types: commodity selling, consultative selling, and institutional selling. Commodity selling is a bit like order taking. The consumer views the broker as a quote shop and the lowest rate is often the primary factor in purchasing. This defines much of the market that sole proprietors and some agencies tend to have to work with in order to operate their businesses. We tend to see a commodity selling paradigm operative among Main Street purchasers and creeping slightly into lower mid-market—basically accounts between $500 commission a year and $40,000–45,000 NCF range. Consultative selling begins after that and extends all the way to an NCF range of perhaps $400,000–500,000 per account, or even further. Consultative selling involves getting to know the prospect—doing diagnostics, assessments, formal discovery, interviews, and constructing an annual or even multiyear stewardship plan and managing it.

Beyond that is institutional selling, which can, as an example, occur when a private equity firm deploys capital into a given entity and as part of that process they wanted someone in particular to manage the insurance program for the entity to which they infused capital. Institutional selling is a completely different paradigm and often exists with larger accounts and/or those where there are infusions of capital—such as private equity, venture capital, or even angel investors.

Why does all this matter? Without industry perspective, producers will tend to lapse into wild goose chases, pursuing business that resides outside both the firm's core business and their own sweet spot. A solid understanding of the industry provides insight into how to compete against others pursuing the same prospect. On a practical level, as a sales leader, you should routinely provide information about the key competitors in your space. Prior to each sales meeting, perform an Internet search on what's happening with some of your key competitors and provide your team with timely information about any new projects, capabilities, resources, or platform extensions your competitors have announced. Routinely feed industry news to your team to provide additional perspective—anything that could reinforce their new business development efforts.

During both specific practice group meetings as well as sales meetings always ask about the best ways to compete against the firms in your local market. This is a great roundtable discussion for your producers that will often generate some real gems that they can use to help each other compete successfully for that business.

How Are You Helping Colleagues Experience Progressively Greater Achievements?

Eventually every producer will hit a stasis point with their book of business if they do not write progressively larger pieces of business year over year. This is the fork in the road that many producers come to and ultimately have to decide for themselves if they want to make adjustments in order to continue the growth of their book. As a leader, you want to encourage the importance of writing progressively larger pieces of business to grow a book sustainably over time, and, of course, help each person on your team do so.

Ultimately a book of business will hit a ceiling when efficiencies of time are inevitably exhausted. Everyone is running as fast as they can with the available time for new business production, but running faster can only take a producer so far because eventually everyone starts spending more time managing the clients that they've already written. Time is precious and needs to be maximized in terms of its efficacy. Progressively greater sales achievement year over year is a function of writing progressively larger cases—and that is enabled by professional development.

As a leader, what can you do? You can certainly encourage joint work; teams tend to buy from teams. The largest account that I wrote by myself when I was a producer was approximately $70,000 NCF. When I worked in a team, the largest account I wrote was $635,000 of NCF. The ability to work within a team and develop that skill is critical to moving up market and writing progressively larger pieces of business over time.

As a leader you can create a developmental curriculum, essentially a twelve-month game plan for your producers. Ask them these questions:

- What would you like to learn that you feel will help you advance your practice?
- What skills would you like to master?
- Would you like to launch a center-of-influence initiative this year?
- Would you like to create a brown bag lunch every other month and have clients and prospects attend it?
- Do you want to learn how to do podcasts?

- Do you want to learn how to do webinars?
- Do you need help learning how to use technology as an accelerator for your practice?

Work with them on what they would like to learn and how they would like to deploy that learning to support their new business development efforts. It's also important for you to encourage exposure to industry thought leadership and acquiring professional designations within the team. This can be especially helpful for developmental producers because a professional designation can go a long way to helping establish credibility with buyers who may be reluctant to do business with anyone they consider to be green.

A critical aspect of helping your colleagues experience progressively greater achievements is keeping an eye on the average case size in your producers' new business pipeline. It must be larger than the average size case in their books of business. If the average size case in their book of business is greater than the average size case in their new business pipeline, then their book is actually shrinking. If the average size case in their new business pipeline is the same as the average size case in their book, they are headed towards a stasis point or have already reached one, meaning a book will remain the same size year over year. If the average size case in their new business pipeline is larger than the average case in their book, great! The book is growing sustainably over time. That's what we all want! Encourage your producers to always keep in mind what the average size case in their book is and compare that to the average size case in their new business pipeline. One of the most important ways to help them grow is to remind them to keep an eye on those metrics.

How Are You Helping Your Colleagues Find Their Authentic Sales Path?

Sales paths will vary by producer tenure, specialty, size of book, and many other attributes and variables. There is no such thing as a one-size-fits-all system applicable to all of your producers. As a leader, it is important to identify your producers' strengths and competencies and to help them find their sweet spot. Help them apply their prospecting efforts toward the type of prospects that have the highest percentage chance for success against other competitors pursuing the same prospects and help them find "imperfections of fit" between a given prospect and the incumbent broker.

Sales initiatives are a great way for leaders to help and support producer efforts. Teach your producers how to develop sales initiatives. They have ideas, they have new things they want to do, and they are seeing things on the ground that can be very good opportunities for an enterprise to provide resources for. In order for them to succeed, you need to teach them how to express what they see, what resources they will need, what kind of budget they will need, and of course an estimate on what kind of return can be expected so that you can rally around that and give them the necessary support to move forward with those initiatives.

Treating your producers by tenure class will unlock the key to many issues relating to successful new business development. The four tenure classes are developmental (first three years in the business), prime (years three to fifteen), career (years fifteen to twenty-five), and sunset (over twenty-five years). Each tenure class will execute differently and need different levels of support, so be cognizant of that.

How Are You Helping Your Colleagues Manage Themselves as Microeconomic Business Units?

Nothing can be more valuable than teaching your producers how to do their own book analysis and their own cash flow projections. Give them some of the tools that they need to navigate their profession within the insurance industry. As we have discussed, sales may be intuitive, but the business of sales is not. To move forward as a highly empowered insurance professional, they have to learn the business side of it. Ask them: If you continue at your annual new business run rate, where will you end up in three years? Five years? Seven years? Are you happy with that? If not, what are we going to do to grow?

You can also teach them fundamentally how their book of business maps out in terms of number of small accounts, middle market, and large market accounts. Teach them how to do a book analysis. Show them how to look at their book of business every year and identify whether they have too many small accounts, whether they can sell more lines of business to their top ten clients, the busy and slow times of the year, and so forth.

It's important to have business tools in order to plan and run a practice. The more you empower a producer, the greater chance there is that they will identify an issue or problem and come to you for help rather than suffer from underperformance. This also takes you out of the business of convincing them that they've got a problem. Better for them to have the tools and resources to properly assess their practice; let them recognize that there is a problem and come to you after they've already recognized that there is something that requires a remedy. That is a much better discussion.

Provide business plans and cash flow templates and teach your producers how to use those. Teach them the economics behind book building: new business run rates, retention rates, general expense, staff compensation, target EBITDA, and so forth. It's okay to talk to them about the costs associated with maintaining client management staff and the general expenses of the company—lease, electricity, IT, and other expenses. This information provides a helpful framework. I would also encourage the following: Every producer should know exactly how much their book needs to grow in order to justify their next account manager. Do yours?

This is important because when people are in the blind and uncertain as to what level the book needs to be in order to justify the next account manager, they tend to feel loaded up and overwhelmed by the hours they are working and as if there is no hope in sight. That may lead them to resign, which is certainly an event to be avoided if at all possible.

Helping your team understand the microeconomic business side is an effective way to empower them to grow as individuals and to become even more valuable team players. By providing effective tools and ongoing education, you may even prevent the need for those painful performance discussions.

Provide a Framework for Progress

It's easy for people to lose focus without a good cadence, no matter how disciplined they are. Everyone gets off track from time to time. That's why it's important to provide structure—so they can't fall too far into a hole.

I've always visualized that being a great sales leader is similar to being the leader of a crew boat with many oars—that person on the back of the boat saying, "Row, row, row." A great sales leader helps everyone to stay coordinated, on cadence, and maintaining rhythm. The team pulls in the same direction yet each individual is in charge of their own oars.

Establishing regular team sales meetings is an important part of this coordination. A standing agenda is key. Remember, without a standing agenda nobody will show up prepared to participate. See Chapter 13 for information about valuable agenda items for sales meetings.

Think of yourself as a lighthouse. Whatever is in the beam of a lighthouse is what is being illuminated in the darkness and visible for others to see clearly. As a leader, your team will look where you look. In the darkness the only thing that anyone can see is whatever is being illuminated by the lighthouse at that given moment of time.

If you are having anemic cross-sell activity, illuminate what needs to be done to increase cross-sell activity in your meetings. If your team is struggling with developing center-of-influence business, then that should be on the agenda of every sales meeting to illuminate that issue. As a leader, it is up to you to see what the issues are and to illuminate them so that individual producers can see them and the business as a whole can grow.

Keep in mind that one-on-one meetings are the best venue for coaching and mentoring. I would encourage you to separate business and performance management from regularly scheduled one-on-one coaching and mentoring meetings in order to keep them collaborative and productive. Perhaps once a month or once a quarter have a business discussion with your producers as a separate dedicated meeting. Go over their book, their new business, their metrics, the operating income they're dropping to the bottom line, and so forth. Those meetings are necessary and can't be neglected. In between those meetings have the coaching, mentoring, and conciliatory discussions with producers during their regular one-on-ones. Nurture them and provide the support they need. Keep their coaching and mentoring discussions completely separate from the business side for the best traction.

———

As a sales leader, you want to be advancing the wealth and prosperity of the producers within your constituency. By helping your colleagues to be good students of the insurance industry, achieve progressively more each year, find their authentic sales path, and understand themselves as microeconomic business units, you are working in the best interests of your team's overall prosperity and helping them advance. In my view, that is what leadership is all about. Teach them, help them, be honest with them, and support them.

Questions to Assess Sales Leadership

- How am I helping my colleagues become dedicated students of the insurance industry?
- How am I helping my colleagues experience progressively greater achievements year over year?
- How am I helping my colleagues find their authentic sales path?
- How am I helping my colleagues manage themselves as microeconomics business units?
- How am I providing a framework to help my colleagues stay on track as they progress toward their goals?

Made in the USA
Middletown, DE
15 January 2020

83209924R00087